Anonymous

Letters

Vol. 2

Anonymous

Letters
Vol. 2

ISBN/EAN: 9783337818555

Printed in Europe, USA, Canada, Australia, Japan

Cover: Foto ©ninafisch / pixelio.de

More available books at **www.hansebooks.com**

JUNIUS.

STAT NOMINIS UMBRA.

VOL. II.

LONDON:
PRINTED BY T. BENSLEY,

FOR VERNOR AND HOOD, J. CUTHELL,
LACKINGTON, ALLEN, AND CO. J. WALKER, R. FAULDER,
OTRIDGE AND SON, AND OGILVY AND SON.

1799.

BOOKS

PRINTED FOR

THE PROPRIETORS OF JUNIUS'S LETTERS.

1. HUDIBRAS, in three parts, corrected and amended, with large Annotations, &c. by Zachary Grey, L.L. D. adorned with Sixteen Copper Plates, engraved by Ridley from Hogarth's Designs; and Twenty-four Head and Tail Pieces, beautifully cut in wood by Nisbet (pupil of Bewick), from humorous Designs by Thurston. In two volumes octavo, boards, 1l. 1s.
A few Copies on Whatman's Royal Vellum Paper, with first Impressions of the Plates, boards, 1l. 15s.

2. The ASIATIC RESEARCHES; or Transactions of the Society instituted in Bengal for inquiring into the History and Antiquities, the Arts, Sciences, and Literature, of Asia. By Sir William Jones, and others. In four volumes octavo, price 2l. 2s. boards, with all the Plates, &c. printed verbatim from the Bengal edition in four volumes quarto.
Vol. I. and II. may be had separate, price 1l. 1l. or gentlemen possessed of the third and fourth volumes in boards, may have them exchanged for complete uniform sets.

3. ZIMMERMAN ON SOLITUDE, translated from the German, with Seven beautiful Plates by Ridley; boards, 6s. 6d.
The same in an elegant Octavo Edition, boards, 8s. 6d.

4. ZIMMERMAN ON SOLITUDE, Volume the Second, uniform with the first, with Four elegant Plates engraved by Ridley; 6s. boards, or octavo 8s. boards.

5. Mrs. DOBSON'S LIFE OF PETRARCH, two volumes octavo, with Eight beautiful Plates; boards, 16s.
The same in Royal Octavo, first Impressions, boards, 1l. 1s.

6. The LETTERS of MARCUS TULLIÙS CICERO to several of his Friends, translated by William Melmoth, Esq. with Remarks and Notes; three volumes octavo, 18s. boards.

7. The ORLANDO FURIOSO of ARIOSTO, in forty-six books, translated by John Hoole; five volumes octavo, with elegant Engravings by Bartolozzi, Heath, Sharp, Caldwell, &c. a new edition, 1l. 12s. 6d. boards.

8. HOOLE'S TASSO'S JERUSALEM DELIVERED, two vols. foolscap octavo, with beautiful Frontispieces, boards, 7s.
The same work in Octavo, boards, 12s.

LIST OF BOOKS.

9. A PHILOSOPHICAL ENQUIRY into the Origin of our Ideas of the SUBLIME and BEAUTIFUL, with an introductory Discourse concerning Taste, and several other Additions. By the late Edmund Burke, Esq. A new edition in octavo, with an elegant Head of the Author; boards, 5s.

10. A COURSE of LECTURES on ELOCUTION; together with two Dissertations on Language, and some other Tracts relative to those subjects. By Thomas Sheridan, A. M. A new edition in octavo, boards, 6s.

11. A General Pronouncing and Explanatory DICTIONARY of the ENGLISH LANGUAGE, for the use of schools, foreigners learning English, &c. in which it has been attempted to improve on the plan of Mr. Sheridan; the discordancies of that celebrated orthoëpist being avoided, and his improprieties corrected. The fourth edition, revised, and considerably enlarged by selections from Ash, Bailey, Barclay, Buchanan, Dyche, Elphinstone, Entick, Fry, Johnson, Johnston, Kenrick, Lemon, Marriott, Martin, Nares, Perry, Rider, Scott, and Walker. By Stephen Jones, Author of the New Biographical Dictionary, and The History of Poland, and Compiler of Dr. Johnson's Table Talk, &c. In one volume octavo, a new edition, enlarged with upwards of 2000 words, boards, 8s. or on fine Royal Paper, boards, 10s. 6d.

The same Work, printed on a fine Crown Paper for the pocket, bound, 3s. 6d. or on fine Vellum Paper, hot-pressed, bound, 4s. 6d.

12. The UNIVERSAL GAZETTEER; being a concise description, alphabetically arranged, of the nations, kingdoms, states, towns, empires, provinces, cities, oceans, seas, harbours, rivers, lakes, canals, mountains, capes, &c. in the known world; the government, manners, and religion of the inhabitants; with the extent, boundaries, and natural productions, manufactures, and curiosities, of the different countries. Containing several thousand places not to be met with in any similar Gazetteer. By John Walker. A new edition, carefully corrected, and considerably enlarged, with Fourteen Maps; boards, 8s. or with coloured Maps, 9s. 6d. boards.—In this edition, besides many other improvements for commercial purposes, the editor has pointed out the post towns of Great Britain and Ireland, not in any similar work.

13. ELEMENTS of GEOGRAPHY, and of NATURAL and CIVIL HISTORY, with Thirty Plates and Maps, correctly engraved. The second edition; boards, 7s.

14. ETUDES de la NATURE, abregé de Bernardin St. Pierre, with an elegant Frontispiece; bound, 4s.

15. STUDIES of NATURE, abridged from the original of Bernardin St. Pierre, with an elegant Frontispiece; bound, 4s.

16. The ECONOMY of HUMAN LIFE. In two parts. By Robert Dodsley. A new edition, with a beautiful Frontispiece; bound, vellum back, 1s.

17. The DEATH of ABEL, translated from the German of Gessner by Mrs. Collier, with Four elegant Plates by Richter; bound, 4s. 6d.

LETTERS OF JUNIUS.

LETTER XXXVII.

TO

THE PRINTER OF THE PUBLIC ADVERTISER.

SIR,   19 March, 1770.

I BELIEVE there is no man, however indifferent about the interests of this country, who will not readily confess that the situation to which we are now reduced, whether it has arisen from the violence of faction, or from an arbitrary system of government, justifies the most melancholy apprehensions, and calls for the exertion of whatever wisdom or vigour is left among us. The king's answer to the remonstrance of the city of London, and the measures since adopted by the ministry, amount to a plain declaration, that the principle on which Mr. Luttrell was seated in the house of commons, is to be supported in all its consequences, and carried to its utmost extent. The same spirit which violated the freedom of election now invades the declaration and bill of rights, and threatens to punish the subject for exercising a privilege hitherto undisputed, of petitioning the crown. The grievances of the people are aggravated by insults; their complaints not merely disregarded, but checked by authority; and every one of those acts against which they remonstrated, confirmed by the king's decisive approbation. At such a moment no honest man will remain silent or inactive. However distinguished by rank or property, in the rights of freedom we are all equal. As we are Englishmen, the least considerable man among us has an interest equal to the proudest nobleman in the laws and constitution of his country, and is equally called upon to make a generous contribution in support of them; whether it be the heart to conceive, the understanding to direct, or the hand to execute. It is a common cause, in which we are all interested, in which we should all be engaged.

The man who deserts it at this alarming crisis is an enemy to his country, and, what I think of infinitely less importance, a traitor to his sovereign. The subject who is truly loyal to the chief magistrate will neither advise nor submit to arbitrary measures. The city of London have given an example which, I doubt not, will be followed by the whole kingdom. The noble spirit of the metropolis is the lifeblood of the state, collected at the heart: from that point it circulates with health and vigour through every artery of the constitution. The time is come when the body of the English people must assert their own cause: conscious of their strength, and animated by a sense of their duty, they will not surrender their birthright to ministers, parliaments, or kings.

The city of London have expressed their sentiments with freedom and firmness; they have spoken truth boldly; and, in whatever light their remonstrance may be represented by courtiers, I defy the most subtle lawyer in this country to point out a single instance in which they have exceeded the truth. Even that assertion, which we are told is most offensive to parliament, in the theory of the English constitution, is strictly true. If any part of the representative body be not chosen by the people, that part vitiates and corrupts the whole. If there be a defect in the representation of the people, that power which alone is equal to the making of the laws in this country is not complete, and the acts of parliament under that circumstance are not the acts of a pure and entire legislature. I speak of the theory of our constitution; and, whatever difficulties or inconveniences may attend the practice, I am ready to maintain, that, as far as the fact deviates from the principle, so far the practice is vicious and corrupt. I have not heard a question raised upon any other part of the remonstrance. That the principle on which the Middlesex election was determined is more pernicious in its effects than either the levying of ship-money by Charles the First, or the suspending power assumed by his son, will hardly be disputed by any man who understands or wishes well to the English constitution. It is not an act of open violence done by the king, or any direct or palpable breach of the laws attempted by his minister, that can ever endanger the liberties of this country. Against such a king or minister the people would immediately take the alarm, and all the parties unite to oppose him. The laws may be grossly violated in particular instances without any direct attack upon the whole system. Facts of that kind stand alone; they are attributed to necessity, not defended by principle. We can never be really in danger, until the forms of parliament are made use of to destroy the substance of our civil and political liberties; until parliament itself betrays its trust, by contributing to establish new principles of government, and employing the very weapons committed to it by the collective body to stab the constitution.

As for the terms of the remonstrance, I presume it will not be affirmed, by any person less polished than a gentleman usher, that this is a season for compliments. Our gracious king indeed is abundantly civil to himself. Instead of an answer to a petition, his majesty very gracefully pronounces his own panegyric; and I confess, that as far as his personal behaviour, or the royal purity of his intentions, is concerned, the truth of those declarations which the minister has drawn up for his master cannot decently be disputed. In every other respect, I affirm, that they are absolutely unsupported either in argument or fact. I must add too, that supposing the speech were otherwise unexceptionable, it is not a direct answer to the petition of the city. His majesty is pleased to say, that he is always ready to receive the requests of his subjects, yet the sheriffs were twice sent back with an excuse, and it was certainly debated in council whether or no the magistrates of the city of London should be admitted to an audience. Whether the remonstrance be or be not injurious to parliament, is the very question between the parliament and the people, and such a question as cannot be decided by the assertion of a third party, however respectable. That the petitioning for a dissolution of parliament is irreconcileable with the principles of the constitution, is a new doctrine. His majesty perhaps has not been informed, that the house of commons themselves have, by a formal resolution, admitted it to be the right of the subject. His majesty proceeds to assure us that he has made the laws the rule of his conduct. Was it in ordering or permitting his ministers to apprehend Mr. Wilkes by a general warrant? Was it in suffering his ministers to revive the obsolete maxim of nullum tempus to rob the duke of Portland of his property, and thereby give a decisive turn to a county election? Was it in erecting a chamber consultation of surgeons, with authority to examine into and supersede the legal verdict of a jury? Or did his majesty consult the laws of this country when he permitted his secretary of state to declare, that whenever the civil magistrate is trifled with, a military force must be sent for, without the delay of a moment, and effectually employed? Or was it in the barbarous exactness with which this illegal, inhuman doctrine was carried into execution? If his majesty had recollected these facts, I think he would never have said, at least with any reference to the measures of his government, that he had made the laws the rule of his conduct. To talk of preserving the affections, or relying on the support, of his subjects, while he continues to act upon these principles, is indeed paying a compliment to their loyalty which I hope they have too much spirit and understanding to deserve.

His majesty, we are told, is not only punctual in the performance of his own duty, but careful not to assume any of those powers which the constitution has placed in other hands. Admitting this last assertion to be strictly true, it is no way to the purpose. The city of London have not desired the king to assume a power placed in other hands. If they had, I should hope to see the person who dared to present such a petition immediately impeached. They solicit their sovereign to exert that constitutional authority which the laws have vested in him for the benefit of his subjects. They call upon him to make use of his lawful prerogative in a case which our laws evidently supposed might happen, since they have provided for it by trusting the sovereign with a discretionary power to dissolve the parliament. This request will, I am confident, be supported by remonstrances from all parts of the kingdom. His majesty will find at last that this is the sense of his people, and that it is not his interest to support either ministry or parliament at the hazard of a breach with the collective body of his subjects. That he is the king of a free people is indeed his greatest glory. That he may long continue the king of a free people is the second wish that animates my heart. The first is, that the people may be free[a].

JUNIUS.

[a] When his majesty had done reading his speech, the lord mayor, &c. had the honour of kissing his majesty's hand; after which, as they were withdrawing, his majesty turned round to his courtiers, and burst out a laughing.

Nero fiddled, while Rome was burning.   JOHN HORNE.

LETTER XXXVIII.

TO

THE PRINTER OF THE PUBLIC ADVERTISER.

SIR, 3 April, 1770.

In my last letter I offered you my opinion of the truth and propriety of his majesty's answer to the city of London, considering it merely as the speech of a minister, drawn up in his own defence, and delivered, as usual, by the chief magistrate. I would separate, as much as possible, the king's personal character and behaviour from the acts of the present government. I wish it to be understood that his majesty had in effect no more concern in the substance of what he said than sir James Hodges had in the remonstrance, and that as sir James, in virtue of his office, was obliged to speak the sentiments of the people, his majesty might think himself bound, by the same official obligation, to give a graceful utterance to the sentiments of his minister. The cold formality of a well repeated lesson is widely distant from the animated expression of the heart.

This distinction, however, is only true with respect to the measure itself. The consequences of it reach beyond the minister, and materially affect his majesty's honour. In their own nature they are formidable enough to alarm a man of prudence, and disgraceful enough to afflict a man of spirit. A subject whose sincere attachment to his majesty's person and family is founded upon rational principles, will not, in the present conjuncture, be scrupulous of alarming or even of afflicting his sovereign. I know there is another sort of loyalty of which his majesty has had plentiful experience. When the loyalty of tories, jacobites, and Scotchmen, has once taken possession of an unhappy prince, it seldom leaves him without accomplishing his destruction. When the poison of their doctrines has tainted the natural benevolence of his disposition, when their insidious counsels have corrupted the stamina of his government, what antidote can restore him to his political health and honour, but the firm sincerity of his English subjects?

It has not been usual in this country, at least since

the days of Charles the First, to see the sovereign personally at variance, or engaged in a direct altercation, with his subjects. Acts of grace and indulgence are wisely appropriated to him, and should constantly be performed by himself. He never should appear but in an amiable light to his subjects. Even in France, as long as any ideas of a limited monarchy were thought worth preserving, it was a maxim, that no man should leave the royal presence discontented. They have lost or renounced the moderate principles of their government, and now, when their parliaments venture to remonstrate, the tyrant comes forward, and answers absolutely for himself. The spirit of their present constitution requires that the king should be feared, and the principle, I believe, is tolerably supported by the fact. But in our political system the theory is at variance with the practice, for the king should be beloved. Measures of greater severity may indeed, in some circumstances, be necessary; but the minister who advises should take the execution and odium of them entirely upon himself. He not only betrays his master, but violates the spirit of the English constitution, when he exposes the chief magistrate to the personal hatred or contempt of his subjects. When we speak of the firmness of government, we mean an uniform system of measures, deliberately adopted and resolutely maintained by the servants of the crown, not a peevish asperity in the language or behaviour of the sovereign. The government of a weak irresolute monarch may be wise, moderate, and firm; that of an obstinate, capricious prince, on the contrary, may be feeble, undetermined, and relaxed. The reputation of public measures depends upon the minister, who is responsible, not upon the king, whose private opinions are not supposed to have any weight against the advice of his counsel, whose personal authority should therefore never be interposed in public affairs. This, I believe, is true constitutional doctrine. But for a moment let us suppose it false. Let it be taken for granted, that an occasion may arise in which a king of England shall be compelled to take upon himself the ungrateful office of rejecting the petitions and censuring the conduct of his subjects; and let the city remonstrance be supposed to have created so extraordinary an occasion. On this principle, which I presume no friend of administration will dispute, let the wisdom and spirit of the ministry be examined. They advise the king to hazard his dignity by a positive declaration of his own sentiments; they suggest to him a language full of severity and reproach. What follows? When his majesty had taken so decisive a part in support of his ministry and parliament, he had a right to expect from them a reciprocal demonstration of firmness in their own cause, and of their zeal for his honour. He had reason to expect (and such, I doubt not, were the blustering promises of lord North) that the persons whom he had been advised to charge with having failed in their respect to him, with having injured parliament, and violated the principles of the constitution, should not have been permitted to escape without some severe marks of the displeasure and vengeance of parliament. As the matter stands, the minister, after placing his sovereign in the most unfavourable light to his subjects, and after attempting to fix the ridicule and odium of his own precipitate measures upon the royal character, leaves him a solitary figure upon the scene, to recall, if he can, or to compensate, by future compliances, for one unhappy demonstration of ill-supported firmness, and ineffectual resentment. As a man of spirit, his majesty cannot but be sensible, that the lofty terms in which he was persuaded to reprimand the city, when united with the silly conclusion of the business, resemble the pomp of a mock-tragedy, where the most pathetic sentiments, and even the sufferings of the hero, are calculated for derision.

Such has been the boasted firmness and consistency of a minister [b] whose appearance in the house of commons was thought essential to the king's service; whose presence was to influence every division; who had a voice to persuade, an eye to penetrate, a gesture to command. The reputation of these great qualities has been fatal to his friends. The little dignity of Mr. Ellis has been committed. The mine was sunk, combustibles provided, and Welbore Ellis, the Guy Faux of the fable, waited only for the signal of command. All of a sudden the country gentlemen discover how grossly they have been deceived; the minister's heart fails him, the grand plot is defeated in a moment, and poor Mr. Ellis and his motion taken into custody. From the event of Friday last, one would imagine that some fatality hung over this gentleman. Whether he makes or suppresses a motion, he is equally sure of his dis-

---

[b] This graceful minister is oddly constructed. His tongue is a little too big for his mouth, and his eyes a great deal too big for their sockets. Every part of his person sets natural proportion at defiance. At this present writing his head is supposed to be much too heavy for his shoulders.

grace. But the complexion of the times will suffer no man to be vice-treasurer of Ireland with impunity.[c]

I do not mean to express the smallest anxiety for the minister's reputation. He acts separately for himself, and the most shameful inconsistency may perhaps be no disgrace to him. But when the sovereign, who represents the majesty of the state, appears in person, his dignity should be supported. The occasion should be important; the plan well considered; the execution steady and consistent. My zeal for his majesty's real honour compels me to assert, that it has been too much the system of the present reign to introduce him personally, either to act for, or to defend his servants. They persuade him to do what is properly their business, and desert

[c] About this time the courtiers talked of nothing but a bill of pains and penalties against the lord mayor and sheriffs, or impeachment at the least. Little mannikin Ellis told the king that, if the business were left to his management, he would engage to do wonders. It was thought very odd that a motion of so much importance should be entrusted to the most contemptible little piece of machinery in the whole kingdom. His honest zeal however was disappointed. The minister took fright, and at the very instant that little Ellis was going to open, sent him an order to sit down. All their magnanimous threats ended in a ridiculous vote of censure, and a still more ridiculous address to the king.

him in the midst of it. Yet this is an inconvenience to which he must for ever be exposed while he adheres to a ministry divided among themselves, or unequal in credit and ability to the great task they have undertaken. Instead of reserving the interposition of the royal personage, as the last resource of government, their weakness obliges them to apply it to every ordinary occasion, and to render it cheap and common in the opinion of the people. Instead of supporting their master, they look to him for support; and for the emoluments of remaining one day more in office, care not how much his sacred character is prostituted and dishonoured.

If I thought it possible for this paper to reach the closet, I would venture to appeal at once to his majesty's judgment. I would ask him, but in the most respectful terms, ' As you are a young man,
' sir, who ought to have a life of happiness in pros-
' pect; as you are a husband; as you are a father
' (your filial duties I own have been religiously per-
' formed); is it bona fide for your interest or your
' honour to sacrifice your domestic tranquillity, and
' to live in a perpetual disagreement with your peo-
' ple, merely to preserve such a chain of beings, as
' North, Barrington, Weymouth, Gower, Ellis,

' Onslow, Rigby, Jerry Dyson, and Sandwich?
' Their very names are a satire upon all govern-
' ment, and I defy the gravest of your chaplains to
' read the catalogue without laughing.'

For my own part, sir, I have always considered addresses from parliament as a fashionable unmeaning formality. Usurpers, idiots, and tyrants, have been successively complimented with almost the same professions of duty and affection. But let us suppose them to mean exactly what they profess. The consequences deserve to be considered. Either the sovereign is a man of high spirit, and dangerous ambition, ready to take advantage of the treachery of his parliament, ready to accept of the surrender they made him of the public liberty; or he is a mild, undesigning prince, who, provided they indulge him with a little state and pageantry, would of himself intend no mischief. On the first supposition, it must soon be decided by the sword, whether the constitution should be lost or preserved. On the second, a prince no way qualified for the execution of a great and hazardous enterprise, and without any determined object in view, may nevertheless be driven into such desperate measures as may lead directly to his ruin, or disgrace himself by a shameful fluctuation between the extremes of violence at one moment, and timidity at another. The minister, perhaps, may have reason to be satisfied with the success of the present hour, and with the profits of his employment. He is the tenant of the day, and has no interest in the inheritance. The sovereign himself is bound by other obligations, and ought to look forward to a superior, a permanent interest. His paternal tenderness should remind him how many hostages he has given to society. The ties of nature come powerfully in aid of oaths and protestations. The father who considers his own precarious state of health, and the possible hazard of a long minority, will wish to see the family estate free and unincumbered[d]. What is the dignity of the crown, though it were really maintained; what is the honour of parliament, supposing it could exist without any foundation of integrity and justice; or what is the vain reputation of firmness, even if the scheme of the government were uniform and consistent, compared with the heartfelt affections of the people, with the happiness and security of the royal family, or even with the grateful acclamations

[d] Every true friend of the house of Brunswick sees, with affliction, how rapidly some of the principal branches of the family have dropped off.

of the populace! Whatever style of contempt may be adopted by ministers, or parliaments, no man sincerely despises the voice of the English nation. The house of commons are only interpreters, whose duty it is to convey the sense of the people faithfully to the crown. If the interpretation be false or imperfect, the constituent powers are called upon to deliver their own sentiments. Their speech is rude, but intelligible; their gestures fierce, but full of explanation. Perplexed by sophistries, their honest eloquence rises into action. Their first appeal was to the integrity of their representatives; the second to the king's justice; the last argument of the people, whenever they have recourse to it, will carry more perhaps than persuasion to parliament, or supplication to the throne.

JUNIUS.

LETTER XXXIX.

TO

THE PRINTER OF THE PUBLIC ADVERTISER.

SIR,   28 May, 1770.

WHILE parliament was sitting, it would neither have been safe, nor perhaps quite regular, to offer any opinion to the public upon the justice or wisdom of their proceedings. To pronounce fairly upon their conduct, it was necessary to wait until we could consider, in one view, the beginning, progress, and conclusion, of their deliberations. The cause of the public was undertaken and supported by men whose abilities and united authority, to say nothing of the advantageous ground they stood on, might well be thought sufficient to determine a popular question in favour of the people. Neither was the house of commons so absolutely engaged in defence of the ministry, or even of their own resolutions, but that they might have paid some decent regard to the known disposition of their constituents, and, without any dishonour to their firmness, might have retracted an opinion too hastily adopted, when they saw the alarm it had created, and how strongly it was opposed by the general sense of the nation. The ministry too would have consulted their own immediate interest in making some concession satisfactory to the moderate part of the people. Without touching the fact, they might have consented to guard against, or give up, the dangerous principle on which it was established. In this state of things, I think it was highly improbable, at the beginning of the session, that the complaints of the people upon a matter which, in their apprehension at least, immediately affected the life of the constitution, would be treated with as much contempt by their own representatives, and by the house of lords, as they had been by the other branch of the legislature. Despairing of their integrity, we had a right to expect something from their prudence, and something from their fears. The duke of Grafton certainly did not foresee to what an extent the corruption of a parliament might be carried. He thought, perhaps, that there still was some portion of shame or virtue left in the majority of the house of commons, or that there was a line in public prostitution beyond which they would scruple to proceed. Had the young man been a little more practised in the world, or had he ventured to measure the characters of other men by his own, he would not have been so easily discouraged.

The prorogation of parliament naturally calls upon us to review their proceedings, and to consider the condition in which they have left the kingdom. I do not question but they have done what is usually called the king's business, much to his majesty's satisfaction. We have only to lament, that in consequence of a system introduced or revived in the present reign, this kind of merit should be very consistent with the neglect of every duty they owe to the nation. The interval between the opening of the last and close of the former session was longer than usual. Whatever were the views of the minister in deferring the meeting of parliament, sufficient time was certainly given to every member of the house of commons to look back upon the steps he had taken, and the consequences they had produced. The zeal of party, the violence of personal animosities, and the heat of contention, had leisure to subside. From that period, whatever resolution they took was deliberate and prepense. In the preceding session, the dependents of the ministry had affected to believe, that the final determination of the question would have satisfied the nation, or at least put a stop to their complaints; as if the certainty of an evil could diminish the sense of it, or the nature of injustice could be altered by decision. But they found the people of England were in a temper very distant from submission; and, although it was contended that the house of commons could not themselves reverse a resolution which had the force and effect of a judicial sentence, there were other constitutional expedients which would have given a security against any similar attempts for the future. The general proposition, in which the whole country had an interest, might have been reduced to a particular fact, in which Mr. Wilkes and Mr. Luttrell would alone have been concerned. The house of lords might interpose; the king might dissolve the parliament; or, if every other resource failed, there still lay a grand constitutional writ of error, in behalf of the people, from the decision of one court to the wisdom of the whole legislature. Every one of these remedies has been successively attempted. The people performed their part with dignity, spirit, and perseverance. For many months his majesty heard nothing from his people but the language of complaint and resentment; unhappily for this country, it was the daily triumph of his courtiers, that he heard it with indifference approaching to contempt.

The house of commons having assumed a power unknown to the constitution, were determined not merely to support it in the single instance in question, but to maintain the doctrine in its utmost extent, and to establish the fact as a precedent in law, to be applied in whatever manner his majesty's servants should hereafter think fit. Their proceedings upon this occasion are a strong proof that a decision, in the first instance illegal and unjust, can only be supported by a continuation of falsehood and injustice. To support their former resolutions, they were obliged to violate some of the best known and established rules of the house. In one instance they went so far as to declare, in open defiance of truth and common sense, that it was not the rule of the house to divide a complicated question at the request of a member[e]. But after trampling upon the laws of the land, it was not wonderful that they should

[e] This extravagant resolution appears in the votes of the house; but, in the minutes of the committees, the instances of resolutions contrary to law and truth, or of refusals to acknowledge law and truth when proposed to them, are innumerable.

treat the private regulations of their own assembly with equal disregard. The speaker being young in office, began with pretended ignorance, and ended with deciding for the ministry. We were not surprised at the decision; but he hesitated and blushed at his own baseness, and every man was astonished [f].

The interest of the public was vigorously supported in the house of lords. Their right to defend the constitution against an incroachment of the other estates, and the necessity of exerting it at this period, was urged to them with every argument that could be supposed to influence the heart or the understanding. But it soon appeared, that they had already taken their part, and were determined to support the house of commons, not only at the ex-

[f] When it was a measure of government to destroy Mr. Wilkes, and when for this purpose it was necessary to run down privilege, sir Fletcher Norton, with his usual prostituted effrontery, assured the house of commons, that he should regard one of their votes no more than a resolution of so many drunken porters. This is the very lawyer whom Ben Jonson describes in the following lines:

' Gives forked counsel; takes provoking gold,
' On either hand, and puts it up.
' So wise, so grave, of so perplex'd a tongue,
' And loud withal, that would not wag, nor scarce
' Lie still without a fee.'

pence of truth and decency, but even by a surrender of their own most important rights. Instead of performing that duty which the constitution expected from them, in return for the dignity and independence of their station, in return for the hereditary share it has given them in the legislature, the majority of them made common cause with the other house in oppressing the people, and established another doctrine as false in itself, and, if possible, more pernicious to the constitution than that on which the Middlesex election was determined. By resolving, ' that they had no right to impeach a judgment of ' the house of commons in any case whatsoever, ' where that house has a competent jurisdiction,' they in effect gave up that constitutional check and reciprocal control of one branch of the legislature over the other, which is perhaps the greatest and most important object provided for by the division of the whole legislative power into three estates; and now let the judicial decisions of the house of commons be ever so extravagant, let their declarations of the law be ever so flagrantly false, arbitrary, and oppressive to the subject, the house of lords have imposed a slavish silence upon themselves; they cannot interpose, they cannot protect the subject, they cannot defend the laws of their country. A concession so extraordinary in itself, so contradictory to the principles of their own institution, cannot but alarm the most unsuspecting mind. We may well conclude, that the lords would hardly have yielded so much to the other house without the certainty of a compensation, which can only be made to them at the expence of the people [g]. The arbitrary power they have assumed of imposing fines, and committing during pleasure, will now be exercised in its full extent. The house of commons are too much in their debt to question or interrupt their proceedings. The crown too, we may be well assured, will lose nothing in this new distribution of power. After declaring, that to petition for a dissolution of parliament is irreconcileable with the principles of the constitution, his majesty has reason to expect that some extraordinary compliment will be returned to the royal prerogative. The three branches of the legislature seem to treat their separate rights and interests as the Roman triumvirs did their friends. They reciprocally sacrifice them to the animosities of

[g] The man who resists and overcomes this iniquitous power assumed by the lords, must be supported by the whole people. We have the laws of our side, and want nothing but an intrepid leader. When such a man stands forth, let the nation look to it. It is not his cause, but our own.

each other, and establish a detestable union among themselves, upon the ruin of the laws and liberty of the commonwealth.

Through the whole proceedings of the house of commons in this session, there is an apparent, a palpable consciousness of guilt, which has prevented their daring to assert their own dignity where it has been immediately and grossly attacked. In the course of Dr. Musgrave's examination, he said every thing that can be conceived mortifying to individuals, or offensive to the house. They voted his information frivolous, but they were awed by his firmness and integrity, and sunk under it [h]. The terms in which the sale of a patent to Mr. Hine were communicated to the public naturally called for a parliamentary inquiry. The integrity of the house of commons was directly impeached; but they had not courage to move in their own vindication, because the inquiry would have been fatal to colonel Burgoyne and the duke of Grafton. When sir

[h] The examination of this firm, honest man, is printed for Almon. The reader will find it a most curious, and a most interesting tract. Doctor Musgrave, with no other support but truth, and his own firmness, resisted and overcame the whole house of commons.

George Savile branded them with the name of traitors to their constituents, when the lord mayor, the sheriffs, and Mr. Trecothick, expressly avowed and maintained every part of the city remonstrance, why did they tamely submit to be insulted? Why did they not immediately expel those refractory members? Conscious of the motives on which they had acted, they prudently preferred infamy to danger, and were better prepared to meet the contempt, than to rouse the indignation of the whole people. Had they expelled those five members, the consequences of the new doctrine of incapacitation would have come immediately home to every man. The truth of it would then have been fairly tried, without any reference to Mr. Wilkes's private character, or the dignity of the house, or the obstinacy of one particular county. These topics, I know, have had their weight with men who, affecting a character of moderation, in reality consult nothing but their own immediate ease; who are weak enough to acquiesce under a flagrant violation of the laws, when it does not directly touch themselves, and care not what injustice is practised upon a man whose moral character they piously think themselves obliged to condemn. In any other circumstances, the house of commons must have forfeited all credit and dignity if, after such gross provocation, they had permitted those five gentlemen to sit any longer among them. We should then have seen and felt the operation of a precedent which is represented to be perfectly barren and harmless. But there is a set of men in this country whose understandings measure the violation of law by the magnitude of the instance, not by the important consequences which flow directly from the principle; and the minister, I presume, did not think it safe to quicken their apprehensions too soon. Had Mr. Hampden reasoned and acted like the moderate men of these days, instead of hazarding his whole fortune in a law-suit with the crown, he would have quietly paid the twenty shillings demanded of him, the Stuart family would probably have continued upon the throne, and at this moment the imposition of ship-money would have been an acknowledged prerogative of the crown.

What then has been the business of the session after voting the supplies, and confirming the determination of the Middlesex election? The extraordinary prorogation of the Irish parliament, and the just discontents of that kingdom, have been passed by without notice. Neither the general situation of our colonies, nor that particular distress which forced the inhabitants of Boston to take up arms in their defence, have been thought worthy of a moment's consideration. In the repeal of those acts which were most offensive to America, the parliament have done every thing but remove the offence. They have relinquished the revenue, but judiciously taken care to preserve the contention. It is not pretended that the continuation of the tea duty is to produce any direct benefit whatsoever to the mother country. What is it then but an odious, unprofitable exertion of a speculative right, and fixing a badge of slavery upon the Americans, without service to their masters! But it has pleased God to give us a ministry and a parliament who are neither to be persuaded by argument, nor instructed by experience.

Lord North, I presume, will not claim an extraordinary merit from any thing he has done this year in the improvement or application of the revenue. A great operation, directed to an important object, though it should fail of success, marks the genius and elevates the character of a minister. A poor contracted understanding deals in little schemes, which dishonour him if they fail, and do him no credit when they succeed. Lord North had fortunately the means in his possession of reducing all the four per cents at once. The failure of his first enterprize in finance is not half so disgraceful to his reputation as a minister, as the enterprise itself is injurious to the public. Instead of striking one decisive blow, which would have cleared the market at once, upon terms proportioned to the price of the four per cents six weeks ago, he has tampered with a pitiful portion of a commodity which ought never to have been touched but in gross; he has given notice to the holders of that stock, of a design formed by government to prevail upon them to surrender it by degrees, consequently has warned them to hold up and inhance the price; so that the plan of reducing the four per cents must either be dropped entirely, or continued with an increasing disadvantage to the public. The minister's sagacity has served to raise the value of the thing he means to purchase, and to sink that of the three per cents, which it is his purpose to sell. In effect, he has contrived to make it the interest of the proprietor of four per cents to sell out and buy three per cents in the market, rather than subscribe his stock upon any terms that can possibly be offered by government.

The state of the nation leads us naturally to consider the situation of the king. The prorogation of parliament has the effect of a temporary dissolution. The odium of measures adopted by the collective body sits lightly upon the separate members who composed it. They retire into summer quarters, and rest from the disgraceful labours of the campaign. But as for the sovereign, it is not so with him. He has a permanent existence in this country; he cannot withdraw himself from the complaints, the discontents, the reproaches of his subjects. They pursue him to his retirement, and invade his domestic happiness, when no address can be obtained from an obsequious parliament to encourage or console him. In other times, the interest of the king and people of England was, as it ought to be, entirely the same. A new system has not only been adopted in fact, but professed upon principle. Ministers are no longer the public servants of the state, but the private domestics of the sovereign. One particular class of men[1] are permitted to call themselves the king's friends, as if the body of the people were the king's enemies; or as if his majesty looked for a resource or consolation in

[1] 'An ignorant, mercenary, and servile crew; unanimous in
'evil, diligent in mischief, variable in principles, constant to flattery,
'talkers for liberty, but slaves to power; styling themselves the
'court party, and the prince's only friends.'—DAVENANT.

the attachment of a few favourites, against the general contempt and detestation of his subjects. Edward and Richard the Second made the same distinction between the collective body of the people, and a contemptible party who surrounded the throne. The event of their mistaken conduct might have been a warning to their successors. Yet the errors of those princes were not without excuse. They had as many false friends as our present gracious sovereign, and infinitely greater temptations to seduce them. They were neither sober, religious, nor demure. Intoxicated with pleasure, they wasted their inheritance in pursuit of it. Their lives were like a rapid torrent, brilliant in prospect, though useless or dangerous in its course. In the dull, unanimated existence of other princes, we see nothing but a sickly, stagnant water, which taints the atmosphere without fertilizing the soil. The morality of a king is not to be measured by vulgar rules. His situation is singular. There are faults which do him honour, and virtues that disgrace him. A faultless, insipid equality in his character, is neither capable of vice nor virtue in the extreme; but it secures his submission to those persons whom he has been accustomed to respect, and makes him a dangerous instrument of their ambition. Secluded from the world, attached from his infancy to one set of persons, and one set of ideas, he can neither open his heart to new connexions, nor his mind to better information. A character of this sort is the soil fittest to produce that obstinate bigotry in politics and religion, which begins with a meritorious sacrifice of the understanding, and finally conducts the monarch and the martyr to the block.

At any other period, I doubt not, the scandalous disorders which have been introduced into the government of all the dependencies in the empire would have roused the attention of the public. The odious abuse and prostitution of the prerogative at home, the unconstitutional employment of the military, the arbitrary fines and commitments by the house of lords and court of king's bench, the mercy of a chaste and pious prince extended cheerfully to a wilful murderer, because that murderer is the brother of a common prostitute [k], would, I think, at any other time, have excited universal indignation. But the daring attack upon the constitution, in the Middlesex election, makes us callous and indifferent to

[k] Miss Kennedy; her brothers were condemned for the murder of a watchman. The interest of her paramours procured them a pardon.

inferior grievances. No man regards an eruption upon the surface when the noble parts are invaded, and he feels a mortification approaching to his heart. The free election of our representatives in parliament comprehends, because it is, the source and security of every right and privilege of the English nation. The ministry have realized the compendious ideas of Caligula. They know that the liberty, the laws, and property of an Englishman have in truth but one neck, and that to violate the freedom of election strikes deeply at them all.

JUNIUS.

W. Ridley sculp.

Lord North

Published by Vernor & Hood 31 Poultry, April 1, 1798.

LETTER XL.

TO

LORD NORTH.

MY LORD, 22 August, 1770.

Mr. Luttrell's services were the chief support and ornament of the duke of Grafton's administration. The honour of rewarding them was reserved for your lordship. The duke, it seems, had contracted an obligation he was ashamed to acknowledge, and unable to acquit. You, my lord, had no scruples. You accepted the succession with all its incumbrances, and have paid Mr. Luttrell his legacy, at the hazard of ruining the estate.

When this accomplished youth declared himself the champion of government, the world was busy in inquiring what honours or emoluments could be a sufficient recompense to a young man of his rank and fortune, for submitting to mark his entrance into life with the usual contempt and detestation of his country. His noble father had not been so precipitate. To vacate his seat in parliament; to intrude upon a county in which he had no interest or connexion; to possess himself of another man's right, and to maintain it in defiance of public shame as well as justice, bespoke a degree of zeal or of depravity, which all the favour of a pious prince could hardly requite. I protest, my lord, there is in this young man's conduct a strain of prostitution which, for its singularity, I cannot but admire. He has discovered a new line in the human character; he has degraded even the name of Luttrell, and gratified his father's most sanguine expectations.

The duke of Grafton, with every possible disposition to patronize this kind of merit, was contented with pronouncing colonel Luttrell's panegyric. The gallant spirit, the disinterested zeal of the young adventurer, were echoed through the house of lords. His grace repeatedly pledged himself to the house, as an evidence of the purity of his friend Mr. Luttrell's intentions, that he had engaged without any prospect of personal benefit, and that the idea of compensation would mortally offend him[1]. The noble duke could hardly be in earnest; but he had lately quitted his employment, and began to think it necessary to take some care of his reputation. At that very moment the Irish negociation was probably begun. Come forward, thou worthy representative of lord Bute, and tell this insulted country who advised the king to appoint Mr. Luttrell adjutant-general to the army in Ireland. By what management was colonel Cunninghame prevailed on to resign his employment, and the obsequious Gisborne to accept of a pension for the government of Kinsale?[m] Was it an original stipulation with the princess of Wales, or does he owe his preferment to your lordship's partiality, or to the duke of Bedford's friendship? My lord, though it may not be

[1] He now says that his great object is the rank of colonel, and that he will have it.

[m] This infamous transaction ought to be explained to the public. Colonel Gisborne was quarter-master-general in Ireland. Lord Townshend persuades him to resign to a Scotch officer, one Fraser, and gives him the government of Kinsale. Colonel Cunninghame was adjutant-general in Ireland. Lord Townshend offers him a pension, to induce him to resign to Luttrell. Cunninghame treats the

possible to trace this measure to its source, we can follow the stream, and warn the country of its approaching destruction. The English nation must be roused, and put upon its guard. Mr. Luttrell has already shewn us how far he may be trusted whenever an open attack is to be made upon the liberties of this country. I do not doubt that there is a deliberate plan formed. Your lordship best knows by whom; the corruption of the legislative body on this side, a military force on the other, and then, Farewell to England! It is impossible that any minister shall dare to advise the king to place such a man as Luttrell in the confidential post of adjutant-general, if there were not some secret purpose in view which only such a man as Luttrell is fit to promote. The insult offered to the army in general is as gross as the outrage intended to the people of England. What! lieutenant-colonel Luttrell adjutant-general of an army of sixteen thousand men! One would think his majesty's campaigns at Blackheath and Wimbledon might have taught him bet-

offer with contempt. What's to be done? poor Gisborne must move once more. He accepts of a pension of 500 l. a year, until a government of greater value shall become vacant. Colonel Cunninghame is made governor of Kinsale; and Luttrell, at last, for whom the whole machinery is put in motion, becomes adjutant-general, and in effect takes the command of the army in Ireland.

ter. I cannot help wishing general Harvey joy of a colleague who does so much honour to the employment. But, my lord, this measure is too daring to pass unnoticed, too dangerous to be received with indifference or submission. You shall not have time to new-model the Irish army. They will not submit to be garbled by colonel Luttrell. As a mischief to the English constitution (for he is not worth the name of enemy) they already detest him. As a boy, impudently thrust over their heads, they will receive him with indignation and contempt. As for you, my lord, who perhaps are no more than the blind, unhappy instrument of lord Bute and her royal highness the princess of Wales, be assured that you shall be called upon to answer for the advice which has been given, and either discover your accomplices, or fall a sacrifice to their security.

JUNIUS.

LETTER XLI.

TO

THE RIGHT HONOURABLE LORD MANSFIELD.

MY LORD,   14 November, 1770.

THE appearance of this letter will attract the curiosity of the public, and command even your lordship's attention. I am considerably in your debt, and shall endeavour, once for all, to balance the account. Accept of this address, my lord, as a prologue to more important scenes in which you will probably be called upon to act or suffer.

You will not question my veracity, when I assure you that it has not been owing to any particular respect for your person that I have abstained from you so long. Besides the distress and danger with which the press is threatened when your lordship is party, and the party is to be judge, I confess I have been deterred by the difficulty of the task. Our language has no term of reproach, the mind has no idea of detestation, which has not already been happily applied to you, and exhausted. Ample justice has been done by abler pens than mine to the separate merits of your life and character. Let it be my humble office to collect the scattered sweets, till their united virtue tortures the sense.

Permit me to begin with paying a just tribute to Scotch sincerity wherever I find it. I own I am not apt to confide in the professions of gentlemen of that country, and when they smile, I feel an involuntary emotion to guard myself against mischief. With this general opinion of an ancient nation, I always thought it much to your lordship's honour, that, in your early days, you were but little infected with the prudence of your country. You had some original attachments, which you took every proper opportunity to acknowledge. The liberal spirit of youth prevailed over your native discretion. Your zeal in the cause of an unhappy prince was expressed with the sincerity of wine, and some of the solemnities of religion [n]. This, I conceive, is the most amiable point of view in which your character has appeared. Like an honest man, you took that part in politics which might have been expected from your birth, education, country, and connexions. There was something generous in your attachment to the banished house of Stuart. We lament the mistakes of a good man, and do not begin to detest him until he affects to renounce his principles. Why did you not adhere to that loyalty you once professed? Why did you not follow the example of your worthy brother [o]? With him you might have shared in the honour of the pretender's confidence; with him you might have preserved the integrity of your character, and England, I think, might have spared you without regret. Your friends will say, perhaps, that, although you deserted the fortune of your liege lord, you have adhered firmly to the principles which drove his fa-

[n] This man was always a rank jacobite. Lord Ravensworth produced the most satisfactory evidence of his having frequently drank the pretender's health upon his knees.

[o] Confidential secretary to the late pretender. This circumstance confirmed the friendship between the brothers.

ther from the throne; that, without openly supporting the person, you have done essential service to the cause, and consoled yourself for the loss of a favourite family by reviving and establishing the maxims of their government. This is the way in which a Scotchman's understanding corrects the error of his heart. My lord, I acknowledge the truth of the defence, and can trace it through all your conduct. I see through your whole life one uniform plan to enlarge the power of the crown at the expence of the liberty of the subject. To this object your thoughts, words, and actions, have been constantly directed. In contempt or ignorance of the common law of England, you have made it your study to introduce into the court where you preside maxims of jurisprudence unknown to Englishmen. The Roman code, the law of nations, and the opinion of foreign civilians, are your perpetual theme; but who ever heard you mention magna charta or the bill of rights with approbation or respect? By such treacherous arts the noble simplicity and free spirit of our Saxon laws were first corrupted. The Norman conquest was not complete until Norman lawyers had introduced their laws, and reduced slavery to a system. This one leading principle directs your interpretation of the laws, and accounts for your treatment of juries.

It is not in political questions only (for there the courtier might be forgiven), but let the cause be what it may, your understanding is equally on the rack, either to contract the power of the jury, or to mislead their judgment. For the truth of this assertion, I appeal to the doctrine you delivered in lord Grosvenor's cause. An action for criminal conversation being brought by a peer against a prince of the blood, you were daring enough to tell the jury, that, in fixing the damages, they were to pay no regard to the quality or fortune of the parties; that it was a trial between A. and B., that they were to consider the offence in a moral light only, and give no greater damages to a peer of the realm than to the meanest mechanic. I shall not attempt to refute a doctrine which, if it was meant for law, carries falsehood and absurdity upon the face of it; but, if it was meant for a declaration of your political creed, is clear and consistent. Under an arbitrary government, all ranks and distinctions are confounded. The honour of a nobleman is no more considered than the reputation of a peasant, for, with different liveries, they are equally slaves.

Even in matters of private property, we see the same bias and inclination to depart from the decisions of your predecessors, which you certainly ought to receive as evidence of the common law. Instead of those certain, positive rules, by which the judgment of a court of law should invariably be determined, you have fondly introduced your own unsettled notions of equity and substantial justice. Decisions given upon such principles do not alarm the public so much as they ought, because the consequence and tendency of each particular instance is not observed or regarded. In the mean time the practice gains ground; the court of king's bench becomes a court of equity, and the judge, instead of consulting strictly the law of the land, refers only to the wisdom of the court, and to the purity of his own conscience. The name of Mr. justice Yates will naturally revive in your mind some of those emotions of fear and detestation with which you always beheld him. That great lawyer, that honest man, saw your whole conduct in the light that I do. After years of ineffectual resistance to the pernicious principles introduced by your lordship, and uniformly supported by your humble friends upon the bench, he determined to quit a court whose proceedings and decisions he could neither assent to with honour, nor oppose with success.

The injustice done to an individual [p] is sometimes of service to the public. Facts are apt to alarm us more than the most dangerous principles. The sufferings and firmness of a printer have roused the public attention. You knew and felt that your conduct would not bear a parliamentary inquiry, and you hoped to escape it by the meanest, the basest sacrifice of dignity and consistency that ever was made by a great magistrate. Where was your firmness, where was that vindictive spirit, of which we have seen so many examples, when a man so inconsiderable as Bingley could force you to confess, in the face of this country, that for two years together you had illegally deprived an English subject of his liberty, and that he had triumphed over you at last? Yet I own, my lord, that yours is not an uncommon character. Women, and men like women, are timid, vindictive, and irresolute. Their passions counteract each other, and make the same creature, at one moment hateful, at another contemptible. I fancy, my lord, some time will elapse before you

---

[p] The oppression of an obscure individual gave birth to the famous habeas corpus act of 31 Car. 2. which is frequently considered as another magna charta of the kingdom.—Blackstone, iii. 135.

venture to commit another Englishman for refusing to answer interrogatories [q].

The doctrine you have constantly delivered in cases of libel, is another powerful evidence of a settled plan to contract the legal power of juries, and to draw questions inseparable from fact, within the arbitrium of the court. Here, my lord, you have fortune of your side. When you invade the province of the jury in matter of libel, you, in effect, attack the liberty of the press, and with a single stroke wound two of your greatest enemies. In some instances you have succeeded, because jurymen are too often ignorant of their own rights, and too apt to be awed by the authority of a chief justice. In other criminal prosecutions, the malice of the design is confessedly as much the subject of consideration to a jury, as the certainty of the fact. If a different doctrine prevails in the case of libels, why

[q] Bingley was committed for contempt in not submitting to be examined. He lay in prison two years, until the crown thought the matter might occasion some serious complaint, and therefore he was let out, in the same contumelious state he had been put in, with all his sins about him, unanointed and unanealed. There was much coquetry between the court and the attorney-general about who should undergo the ridicule of letting him escape.—Vide another letter to Almon, p. 189.

should it not extend to all criminal cases? Why not to capital offences? I see no reason (and I dare say you will agree with me that there is no good one) why the life of the subject should be better protected against you than his liberty or property. Why should you enjoy the full power of pillory, fine, and imprisonment, and not be indulged with hanging or transportation? With your lordship's fertile genius and merciful disposition, I can conceive such an exercise of the power you have, as could hardly be aggravated by that which you have not.

But, my lord, since you have laboured (and not unsuccessfully) to destroy the substance of the trial, why should you suffer the form of the verdict to remain? Why force twelve honest men, in palpable violation of their oaths, to pronounce their fellow-subject a guilty man, when, almost at the same moment, you forbid their inquiring into the only circumstance which, in the eye of law and reason, constitutes guilt, the malignity or innocence of his intentions? But I understand your lordship. If you could succeed in making the trial by jury useless and ridiculous, you might then with greater safety introduce a bill into parliament for enlarging the jurisdiction of the court, and extending your favourite trial by interrogatories to every question in which the life or liberty of an Englishman is concerned [r].

Your charge to the jury in the prosecution against Almon and Woodfall contradicts the highest legal authorities, as well as the plainest dictates of reason. In Miller's cause, and still more expressly in that of Baldwin, you have proceeded a step farther, and grossly contradicted yourself. You may know perhaps, though I do not mean to insult you by an appeal to your experience, that the language of truth is uniform and consistent. To depart from it safely requires memory and discretion. In the two last trials, your charge to the jury began, as usual, with assuring them that they had nothing to do with the law, that they were to find the bare fact, and not concern themselves about the legal inferences drawn

---

[r] The philosophical poet doth notably describe the damnable and damned proceedings of the judge of hell.

'Gnossius hæc Rhadamanthus habet durissima regna,
'Castigatque, auditque dolos, subigitque fateri.'

First he punisheth, and then he heareth; and lastly compelleth to confess, and makes and mars laws at his pleasure; like as the centurion, in the holy history, did to St. Paul; for the text saith, ' Cen-
' turio apprehendi Paulum jussit, et se catenis eligari, et tunc inter-
' rogabat, quis fuisset, et quid fecisset.' But good judges and justices abhor these courses.—Coke, 2 Inst. 55.

from it, or the degree of the defendant's guilt. Thus far you were consistent with your former practice. But how will you account for the conclusion? You told the jury, that, ' if, after all, they would take ' upon themselves to determine the law, they might ' do it, but they must be very sure that they deter- ' mined according to law, for it touched their con- ' sciences, and they acted at their peril.' If I understand your first proposition, you meant to affirm, that the jury were not competent judges of the law in the criminal case of a libel; that it did not fall within their jurisdiction; and that, with respect to them, the malice or innocence of the defendant's intentions would be a question coram non judice. But the second proposition clears away your own difficulties, and restores the jury to all their judicial capacities. You make the competence of the *court to depend upon the legality of the decision. In the first instance you deny the power absolutely. In the second you admit the power, provided it be legally exercised. Now, my lord, without pretending to

---

* Directly the reverse of the doctrine he constantly maintained in the house of lords, and elsewhere, upon the decision of the Middlesex election. He invariably asserted that the decision must be legal, because the court was competent; and never could be prevailed on to enter farther into the question.

reconcile the distinctions of Westminster-hall with the simple information of common sense, or the integrity of fair argument, I shall be understood by your lordship, when I assert that, if a jury, or any other court of judicature (for jurors are judges), have no right to enter into a cause, or question of law, it signifies nothing whether their decision be or be not according to law. Their decision is in itself a mere nullity: the parties are not bound to submit to it; and if the jury run any risque of punishment, it is not for pronouncing a corrupt or illegal verdict, but for the illegality of meddling with a point on which they have no legal authority to decide[t].

I cannot quit this subject without reminding your lordship of the name of Mr. Benson. Without offering any legal objection, you ordered a special juryman to be set aside in a cause where the king was prosecutor. The novelty of the fact required explanation. Will you condescend to tell the

[t] These iniquitous prosecutions cost the best of princes six thousand pounds, and ended in the total defeat and disgrace of the prosecutors. In the course of one of them judge Aston had the unparalleled impudence to tell Mr. Morris (a gentleman of unquestionable honour and integrity, and who was then giving his evidence on oath) that he should pay very little regard to any affidavit he should make.

world by what law or custom you were authorised to make a peremptory challenge of a juryman? The parties indeed have this power, and perhaps your lordship, having accustomed yourself to unite the characters of judge and party, may claim it in virtue of the new capacity you have assumed, and profit by your own wrong. The time within which you might have been punished for this daring attempt to pack a jury, is, I fear, elapsed; but no length of time shall erase the record of it.

The mischiefs you have done this country are not confined to your interpretation of the laws. You are a minister, my lord, and, as such, have long been consulted. Let us candidly examine what use you have made of your ministerial influence. I will not descend to little matters, but come at once to those important points on which your resolution was waited for, on which the expectation of your opinion kept a great part of the nation in suspense. A constitutional question arises upon a declaration of the law of parliament, by which the freedom of election and the birthright of the subject were to have been invaded. The king's servants are accused of violating the constitution. The nation is in a ferment. The ablest men of all parties engage in the question, and exert their utmost abilities in the discussion of it. What part has the honest lord Mansfield acted? As an eminent judge of the law, his opinion would have been respected. As a peer, he had a right to demand an audience of his sovereign, and inform him that his ministers were pursuing unconstitutional measures. Upon other occasions, my lord, you have no difficulty in finding your way into the closet. The pretended neutrality of belonging to no party will not save your reputation. In questions merely political, an honest man may stand neuter. But the laws and constitution are the general property of the subject; not to defend is to relinquish; and who is there so senseless as to renounce his share in a common benefit, unless he hopes to profit by a new division of the spoil? As a lord of parliament, you were repeatedly called upon to condemn or defend the new law declared by the house of commons. You affected to have scruples, and every expedient was attempted to remove them. The question was proposed and urged to you in a thousand different shapes. Your prudence still supplied you with evasion; your resolution was invincible. For my own part, I am not anxious to penetrate this solemn secret. I care not to whose wisdom it is intrusted, nor how soon you carry it with you to your grave[u]. You have betrayed your opinion by the very care you have taken to conceal it. It is not from lord Mansfield that we expect any reserve in declaring his real sentiments in favour of government, or in opposition to the people; nor is it difficult to account for the motions of a timid, dishonest heart, which neither has virtue enough to acknowledge truth, nor courage to contradict it. Yet you continue to support an administration which you know is universally odious, and which, on some occasions, you yourself speak of with contempt. You would fain be thought to take no share in government, while, in reality, you are the main spring of the machine. Here too we trace the little, prudential policy of a Scotchman. Instead of acting that open, generous part, which becomes your rank and station, you meanly skulk into the closet, and give your sovereign such advice as you have not spirit to avow or defend. You secretly engross the power, while you decline the title, of minister; and though you dare not be chancellor, you know how to secure the emoluments of the office. Are the seals to be

---

[u] He said in the house of lords, that he believed he should carry his opinion with him to the grave. It was afterwards reported that he had intrusted it, in special confidence, to the ingenious duke of Cumberland.

for ever in commission, that you may enjoy five thousand pounds a year? I beg pardon, my lord; your fears have interposed at last, and forced you to resign. The odium of continuing speaker of the house of lords upon such terms was too formidable to be resisted. What a multitude of bad passions are forced to submit to a constitutional infirmity! But though you have relinquished the salary, you still assume the rights of a minister. Your conduct, it seems, must be defended in parliament. For what other purpose is your wretched friend, that miserable serjeant, posted to the house of commons? Is it in the abilities of a Mr. Leigh to defend the great lord Mansfield? Or is he only the punch of the puppet-shew, to speak as he is prompted, by the chief juggler behind the curtain [x]?

In public affairs, my lord, cunning, let it be ever so well wrought, will not conduct a man honourably through life. Like bad money, it may be current for a time, but it will soon be cried down. It cannot consist with a liberal spirit, though it be sometimes united with extraordinary qualifications. When

---

[x] This paragraph gagged poor Leigh. I really am concerned for the man, and wish it were possible to open his mouth. He is a very pretty orator.

I acknowledge your abilities, you may believe I am sincere. I feel for human nature, when I see a man, so gifted as you are, descend to such vile practices. Yet do not suffer your vanity to console you too soon. Believe me, my good lord, you are not admired in the same degree in which you are detested. It is only the partiality of your friends that balances the defects of your heart with the superiority of your understanding. No learned man, even among your own tribe, thinks you qualified to preside in a court of common law. Yet it is confessed that, under Justinian, you might have made an incomparable prætor. It is remarkable enough, but I hope not ominous, that the laws you understand best, and the judges you affect to admire most, flourished in the decline of a great empire, and are supposed to have contributed to its fall.

Here, my lord, it may be proper for us to pause together. It is not for my own sake that I wish you to consider the delicacy of your situation. Beware how you indulge the first emotions of your resentment. This paper is delivered to the world, and cannot be recalled. The persecution of an innocent printer cannot alter facts nor refute arguments. Do not furnish me with farther materials against yourself. An honest man, like the true religion, appeals to the understanding, or modestly confides in the internal evidence of his conscience. The impostor employs force instead of argument, imposes silence where he cannot convince, and propagates his character by the sword.

JUNIUS.

LETTER XLII.

TO
THE PRINTER OF THE PUBLIC ADVERTISER.

SIR, 30 January, 1771.

If we recollect in what manner the king's friends have been constantly employed, we shall have no reason to be surprised at any condition of disgrace to which the once-respected name of Englishmen may be degraded. His majesty has no cares but such as concern the laws and constitution of this country. In his royal breast there is no room left for resentment, no place for hostile sentiments against the natural enemies of his crown. The system of government is uniform. Violence and oppression at home can only be supported by treachery and submission abroad. When the civil rights of the people are daringly invaded on one side, what have we to expect, but that their political rights should be deserted and betrayed in the same proportion on the other? The plan of domestic policy which has been invariably pursued from the moment of his present majesty's accession, engrosses all the attention of his servants. They know that the security of their places depends upon their maintaining, at any hazard, the secret system of the closet. A foreign war might embarrass, an unfavourable event might ruin the minister, and defeat the deep-laid scheme of policy to which he and his associates owe their employments. Rather than suffer the execution of that scheme to be delayed or interrupted, the king has been advised to make a public surrender, a solemn sacrifice, in the face of all Europe, not only of the interests of his subjects, but of his own personal reputation and of the dignity of that crown which his predecessors have worn with honour. These are strong terms, sir, but they are supported by fact and argument.

The king of Great Britain had been for some years in possession of an island to which, as the ministry themselves have repeatedly asserted, the Spaniards had no claim of right. The importance of the place is not in question. If it were, a better judgment might be formed of it from the opinion of lord Anson and lord Egmont, and from the anxiety of the Spaniards, than from any fallacious insinuations thrown out by men whose interest it is to undervalue that property which they are determined to relinquish. The pretensions of Spain were a subject of negociation between the two courts. They had been discussed, but not admitted. The king of Spain, in these circumstances, bids adieu to amicable negociation, and appeals directly to the sword. The expedition against Port Egmont does not appear to have been a sudden ill-concerted enterprise. It seems to have been conducted not only with the usual military precautions, but in all the forms and ceremonies of war. A frigate was first employed to examine the strength of the place. A message was then sent, demanding immediate possession, in the catholic king's name, and ordering our people to depart. At last a military force appears, and compels the garrison to surrender. A formal capitulation ensues, and his majesty's ship, which might at least have been permitted to bring home his troops immediately, is detained in port twenty days, and her rudder forcibly taken away. This train of facts carries no appearance of the rashness or violence of a Spanish governor. On the contrary, the whole plan seems to have been formed and executed, in consequence of deliberate orders, and a regular instruction from the Spanish court. Mr. Bucarelli is not a pirate, nor has he been treated as such by those who employed him. I feel for the honour of a gentleman, when I affirm that our king owes him a signal reparation. Where will the humiliation of this country end! A king of Great Britain, not contented with placing himself upon a level with the Spanish governor, descends so low as to do a notorious injustice to that governor. As a salvo for his own reputation, he has been advised to traduce the character of a brave officer, and to treat him as a common robber, when he knew with certainty that Mr. Bucarelli had acted in obedience to his orders, and had done no more than his duty. Thus it happens in private life with a man who has no spirit nor sense of honour. One of his equals orders a servant to strike him. Instead of returning the blow to the master, his courage is contented with throwing an aspersion equally false and public upon the character of the servant.

This short recapitulation was necessary to introduce the consideration of his majesty's speech of 13 November, 1770, and the subsequent measures of government. The excessive caution with which the speech was drawn up, had impressed upon me an early conviction, that no serious resentment was thought of, and that the conclusion of the business, whenever it happened, must, in some degree, be dishonourable to England. There appears through the whole speech a guard and reserve in the choice of expression, which shews how careful the ministry were not to embarrass their future projects by any firm or spirited declaration from the throne. When all hopes of peace are lost, his majesty tells his parliament, that he is preparing, not for barbarous war, but (with all his mother's softness) for a different situation. An open hostility, authorised by the Catholic king, is called an act of a governor. This act, to avoid the mention of a regular siege and surrender, passes under the piratical description of seizing by force; and the thing taken is described, not as a part of the king's territory or proper dominion, but merely as a possession, a word expressly chosen in contradistinction to, and exclusion of, the idea of right, and to prepare us for a future surrender both of the right and of the possession. Yet this speech, sir, cautious and equivocal as it is, cannot, by any sophistry, be accommodated to the measures which have since been adopted. It seemed to promise that, whatever might be given up by secret stipulation, some care would be taken to save appearances to the public. The event shews us, that to depart in the minutest article from the nicety and strictness of punctilio, is as dangerous to national honour as to female virtue. The woman who admits of one familiarity, seldom knows where to stop, or what to refuse; and when the counsels of a great country give way in a single instance, when they once are inclined to submission, every step accelerates the rapidity of the descent. The ministry themselves, when they framed the speech, did not foresee that they should ever accede to such an accommodation as they have since advised their master to accept of.

The king says, ' The honour of my crown and ' the rights of my people are deeply affected.' The Spaniard, in his reply, says, ' I give you back pos-' session, but I adhere to my claim of prior right, ' reserving the assertion of it for a more favourable ' opportunity.'

The speech says, ' I made an immediate demand ' of satisfaction, and, if that fails, I am prepared to ' do myself justice.' This immediate demand must have been sent to Madrid on the 12th of September, or in a few days after. It was certainly refused, or ·evaded, and the king has not done himself justice.

When the first magistrate speaks to the nation, some care should be taken of his apparent veracity.

The speech proceeds to say, ' I shall not discon-'tinue my preparations until I have received proper 'reparation for the injury.' If this assurance may be relied on, what an enormous expence is entailed, sine die, upon this unhappy country! Restitution of a possession, and reparation of an injury, are as different in substance as they are in language. The very act of restitution may contain, as in this instance it palpably does, a shameful aggravation of the injury. A man of spirit does not measure the degree of an injury by the mere positive damage he has sustained. He considers the principle on which it is founded; he resents the superiority asserted over him; and rejects with indignation the claim of right which his adversary endeavours to establish, and would force him to acknowledge.

The motives on which the catholic king makes restitution are, if possible, more insolent and disgraceful to our sovereign, than even the declaratory condition annexed to it. After taking four months to consider, whether the expedition was undertaken by his own orders or not, he condescends to disavow

the enterprise, and to restore the island, not from any regard to justice, not from any regard he bears to his Britannic majesty, but merely ' from the per-
' suasion, in which he is, of the pacific sentiments
' of the king of Great Britain.' At this rate, if our king had discovered the spirit of a man, if he had made a peremptory demand of satisfaction, the king of Spain would have given him a peremptory refusal. But why this unseasonable, this ridiculous mention of the king of Great Britain's pacific intentions? Have they ever been in question? Was he the aggressor? Does he attack foreign powers without provocation? Does he even resist when he is insulted? No, sir, if any ideas of strife or hostility have entered his royal mind, they have a very different direction. The enemies of England have nothing to fear from them.

After all, sir, to what kind of disavowal has the king of Spain at last consented? Supposing it made in proper time, it should have been accompanied with instant restitution; and if Mr. Bucarelli acted without orders, he deserved death. Now, sir, instead of immediate restitution, we have a four months of negociation, and the officer whose act is disavowed returns to court, and is loaded with honours.

If the actual situation of Europe be considered, the treachery of the king's servants, particularly of lord North, who takes the whole upon himself, will appear in the strongest colours of aggravation. Our allies were masters of the Mediterranean. The king of France's present aversion from war, and the distraction of his affairs, are notorious. He is now in a state of war with his people. In vain did the catholic king solicit him to take part in the quarrel against us. His finances were in the last disorder, and it was probable that his troops might find sufficient employment at home. In these circumstances, we might have dictated the law to Spain. There are no terms to which she might not have been compelled to submit. At the worst, a war with Spain alone carries the fairest promise of advantage. One good effect at least would have been immediately produced by it. The desertion of France would have irritated her ally, and in all probability have dissolved the family compact. The scene is now fatally changed. The advantage is thrown away. The most favourable opportunity is lost. Hereafter we shall know the value of it. When the French king is reconciled to his subjects; when Spain has completed her preparations; when the collected strength of the house of Bourbon attacks us at once, the king himself will be able to determine upon the wisdom or imprudence of his present conduct. As far as the probability of argument extends, we may safely pronounce, that a conjuncture which threatens the very being of this country, has been wilfully prepared and forwarded by our own ministry. How far the people may be animated to resistance under the present administration, I know not; but this I know with certainty, that, under the present administration, or if any thing like it should continue, it is of very little moment whether we are a conquered nation or not [y].

---

[y] The king's acceptance of the Spanish ambassador's declaration is drawn up in barbarous French, and signed by the earl of Rochford. This diplomatic lord had spent his life in the study and practice of etiquettes, and is supposed to be a profound master of the ceremonies. I will not insult him by any reference to grammar or common sense. If he were even acquainted with the common forms of his office, I should think him as well qualified for it as any man in his majesty's service. The reader is requested to observe lord Rochford's method of authenticating a public instrument. ' En foi de ' quoi, moi sous-signé, un des principaux secretaires d'état S. M. B. ' ai signé la presente de ma signature ordinaire, et icelle fait apposer ' la cachet de nos armes.' In three lines there are no less than seven false concords. But the man does not even know the style of his office; if he had known it, he would have said, ' nous, soussigné ' secretaire d'etat de S. M. B. avons signé, &c.'

Having travelled thus far in the high road of matter of fact, I may now be permitted to wander a little into the field of imagination. Let us banish from our minds the persuasion that these events have really happened in the reign of the best of princes. Let us consider them as nothing more than the materials of a fable in which we may conceive the sovereign of some other country to be concerned. I mean to violate all the laws of probability, when I suppose that this imaginary king, after having voluntarily disgraced himself in the eyes of his subjects, might return to a sense of his dishonour; that he might perceive the snare laid for him by his ministers, and feel a spark of shame kindling in his breast. The part he must then be obliged to act would overwhelm him with confusion. To his parliament he must say, ' I called you toge-
' ther to receive your advice, and have never asked
' your opinion.' To the merchant, ' I have dis-
' tressed your commerce; I have dragged your sea-
' men out of your ships, I have loaded you with a
' grievous weight of insurances.' To the landholder,
' I told you war was too probable, when I was de-
' termined to submit to any terms of accommoda-
' tion; I extorted new taxes from you before it was
' possible they could be wanted, and am now un-

' able to account for the application of them.' 'To the public creditor, ' I have delivered up your for-' tunes a prey to foreigners and to the vilest of your ' fellow-subjects.' Perhaps this repenting prince might conclude with one general acknowledgment to them all—' I have involved every rank of my ' subjects in anxiety and distress, and have nothing ' to offer you in return but the certainty of national ' dishonour, an armed truce, and peace without ' security.'

If these accounts were settled, there would still remain an apology to be made to his navy and to his army. To the first he would say, ' You were ' once the terror of the world. But go back to your ' harbours. A man dishonoured, as I am, has no ' use for your service.' It is not probable that he would appear again before his soldiers, even in the pacific ceremony of a review. But wherever he appeared, the humiliating confession would be extorted from him: ' I have received a blow, and had not ' spirit to resent it. I demanded satisfaction, and ' have accepted a declaration in which the right to ' strike me again is asserted and confirmed.' His countenance at least would speak this language, and even his guards would blush for him.

But to return to our argument. The ministry, it seems, are labouring to draw a line of distinction between the honour of the crown and the rights of the people. This new idea has yet been only started in discourse, for in effect both objects have been equally sacrificed. I neither understand the distinction, nor what use the ministry propose to make of it. The king's honour is that of his people. Their real honour and real interest are the same. I am not contending for a vain punctilio. A clear, unblemished character, comprehends not only the integrity that will not offer, but the spirit that will not submit to, an injury; and whether it belongs to an individual or to a community, it is the foundation of peace, of independence, and of safety. Private credit is wealth; public honour is security. The feather that adorns the royal bird supports his flight. Strip him of his plumage, and you fix him to the earth.

JUNIUS.

LETTER XLIII.

TO

THE PRINTER OF THE PUBLIC ADVERTISER.

SIR, 6 February, 1771.

I HOPE your correspondent Junius is better employed than in answering or reading the criticisms of a newspaper. This is a task, from which, if he were inclined to submit to it, his friends ought to relieve him. Upon this principle, I shall undertake to answer Anti-Junius; more, I believe, to his conviction than to his satisfaction. Not daring to attack the main body of Junius's last letter, he triumphs in having, as he thinks, surprised an out-post, and cut off a detached argument, a mere straggling proposition. But even in this petty warfare he shall find himself defeated.

Junius does not speak of the Spanish nation as the natural enemies of England. He applies that description with the strictest truth and justice to the Spanish court. From the moment when a prince of the house of Bourbon ascended that throne, their whole system of government was inverted, and became hostile to this country. Unity of possession introduced a unity of politics, and Lewis the Fourteenth had reason when he said to his grandson, 'The Pyrenees are removed.' The history of the present century is one continued confirmation of the prophecy.

The assertion ' that violence and oppression at ' home can only be supported by treachery and sub- ' mission abroad,' is applied to a free people, whose rights are invaded, not to the government of a country, where despotic or absolute power is confessedly vested in the prince; and with this application the assertion is true. An absolute monarch, having no points to carry at home, will naturally maintain the honour of his crown in all his transactions with foreign powers. But if we could suppose the sovereign of a free nation possessed with a design to make himself absolute, he would be inconsistent with himself if he suffered his projects to be interrupted or embarrassed by a foreign war; unless that war tended, as in some cases it might, to promote his principal design. Of the three exceptions to this general rule of conduct (quoted by Anti-Junius), that of Oliver Cromwell is the only one in point. Harry the Eighth, by the submission of his parliament, was as absolute a prince as Lewis the Fourteenth. Queen Elizabeth's government was not oppressive to the people; and as to her foreign wars, it ought to be considered that they were unavoidable. The national honour was not in question. She was compelled to fight in defence of her own person and of her title to the crown. In the common cause of selfish policy, Oliver Cromwell should have cultivated the friendship of foreign powers, or at least have avoided disputes with them, the better to establish his tyranny at home. Had he been only a bad man, he would have sacrificed the honour of the nation to the success of his domestic policy. But with all his crimes he had the spirit of an Englishman. The conduct of such a man must always be an exception to vulgar rules. He had abilities sufficient to reconcile contradictions, and to make a great nation at the same moment unhappy and formidable. If it were not for the respect I bear the minister, I could name a man, who, without one grain of understanding, can do half as much as Oliver Cromwell.

Whether or no there be a secret system in the closet, and what may be the object of it, are questions which can only be determined by appearances, and on which every man must decide for himself.

The whole plan of Junius's letter proves that he himself makes no distinction between the real honour of the crown and the real interest of the people. In the climax to which your correspondent objects, Junius adopts the language of the court, and by that conformity gives strength to his argument. He says that ' the king has not only sacri-
' ficed the interests of his people, but (what was
' likely to touch him more nearly) his personal re-
' putation and the dignity of his crown.'

The queries put by Anti-Junius can only be answered by the ministry. Abandoned as they are, I fancy they will not confess that they have for so many years maintained possession of another man's property. After admitting the assertion of the ministry, viz. that the Spaniards had no rightful claim, and after justifying them for saying so, it is his business, not mine, to give us some good reason for their suffering the pretensions of Spain to be a subject of negociation. He admits the facts;—let him reconcile them if he can.

The last paragraph brings us back to the original question, whether the Spanish declaration contains such a satisfaction as the king of Great Britain ought to have accepted. This was the field upon which he ought to have encountered Junius openly and fairly. But here he leaves the argument as no longer defensible. I shall therefore conclude with one general admonition to my fellow-subjects—that when they hear these matters debated, they should not suffer themselves to be misled by general declamations upon the conveniencies of peace, or the miseries of war. Between peace and war, abstractedly, there is not, there cannot be, a question in the mind of a rational being. The real questions are, Have we any security that the peace we have so dearly purchased will last a twelvemonth? and if not, have we, or have we not, sacrificed the fairest opportunity of making war with advantage?

PHILO JUNIUS.

LETTER XLIV.

TO

THE PRINTER OF THE PUBLIC ADVERTISER.

SIR, 22 April, 1771.

To write for profit, without taxing the press; to write for fame, and to be unknown; to support the intrigues of faction, and to be disowned, as a dangerous auxiliary by every party in the kingdom, are contradictions which the minister must reconcile, before I forfeit my credit with the public. I may quit the service, but it would be absurd to suspect me of desertion. The reputation of these papers is an honourable pledge for my attachment to the people. To sacrifice a respected character, and to renounce the esteem of society, requires more than Mr. Wedderburne's resolution; and though in him it was rather a profession than a desertion of his principles, (I speak tenderly of this gentleman, for when treachery is in question, I think we should make allowances for a Scotchman,) yet we have seen him in the house of commons overwhelmed with confusion, and almost bereft of his faculties. But in truth, sir, I have left no room for an accommodation with the piety of St. James's. My offences are not to be redeemed by recantation or repentance. On one side, our warmest patriots would disclaim me as a burthen to their honest ambition. On the other, the vilest prostitution, if Junius could descend to it, would lose its natural merit and influence in the cabinet, and treachery be no longer a recommendation to the royal favour.

The persons who, till within these few years, have been most distinguished by their zeal for high church and prerogative, are now, it seems, the great assertors of the privileges of the house of commons. This sudden alteration of their sentiments or language carries with it a suspicious appearance. When I hear the undefined privileges of the popular branch of the legislature exalted by tories and jacobites, at the expence of those strict rights which are known to the subject and limited by the laws, I cannot but suspect that some mischievous scheme is in agitation to destroy both law and privilege, by opposing them to each other. They who have uniformly denied the power of the whole legislature to alter the descent of the crown, and whose ancestors, in rebellion against his majesty's family, have defended that doctrine at the hazard of their lives, now tell us that privilege of parliament is the only rule of right, and the chief security of the public freedom. I fear, sir, that while forms remain, there has been some material change in the substance of our constitution. The opinions of these men were too absurd to be so easily renounced. Liberal minds are open to conviction. Liberal doctrines are capable of improvement. There are proselytes from atheism, but none from superstition. If their present professions were sincere, I think they could not but be highly offended at seeing a question, concerning parliamentary privilege, unnecessarily started at a season so unfavourable to the house of commons, and by so very mean and insignificant a person as the minor Onslow. They knew that the present house of commons, having commenced hostilities with the people, and degraded the authority of the laws by their own example, were likely enough to be resisted, per fas et nefas. If they were really friends to privilege, they would have thought the question of right too dangerous to be hazarded at this season, and, without the formality of a convention, would have left it undecided.

I have been silent hitherto, though not from that shameful indifference about the interests of society, which too many of us profess, and call moderation. I confess, sir, that I felt the prejudices of my education in favour of a house of commons still hanging about me. I thought that a question between law and privilege could never be brought to a formal decision without inconvenience to the public service, or a manifest diminution of legal liberty; that it ought therefore to be carefully avoided: and when I saw that the violence of the house of commons had carried them too far to retreat, I determined not to deliver a hasty opinion upon a matter of so much delicacy and importance.

The state of things is much altered in this country since it was necessary to protect our representatives against the direct power of the crown. We have nothing to apprehend from prerogative, but every thing from undue influence. Formerly it was the interest of the people, that the privileges of parliament should be left unlimited and undefined. At present it is not only their interest, but I hold it to be essentially necessary to the preservation of the constitution, that the privileges of parliament should be strictly ascertained, and confined within the narrowest bounds the nature of their institution will admit of. Upon the same principle on which I would have resisted prerogative in the last century, I now resist privilege. It is indifferent to me, whether the crown, by its own immediate act, imposes new, and dispenses with old laws; or whether the same arbitrary power produces the same effects through the medium of the house of commons. We trusted our representatives with privileges for their own defence and ours. We cannot hinder their desertion, but we can prevent their carrying over their arms to the service of the enemy. It will be said, that I begin with endeavouring to reduce the argument concerning privilege to a mere question of convenience; that I deny at one moment what I would allow at another; and that to resist the power of a prostituted house of commons may establish a precedent injurious to all future parliaments. To this I answer generally, that human affairs are in no instance governed by strict positive right. If change of circumstances were to have no weight in directing our conduct and opinions, the mutual intercourse of mankind would be nothing more than a contention between positive and equitable right. Society would be a state of war, and law itself would be injustice. On this general ground, it is highly reasonable, that the degree of our submission to privileges which have never been defined by any positive law, should be considered as a question of convenience, and proportioned to the confidence we repose in the integrity of our representatives. As to the injury we may do to any future and more respectable house of commons, I own I am not now sanguine enough to expect a more plentiful harvest of parliamentary virtue in one year than another. Our political climate is severely altered; and, without dwelling upon the depravity of modern times, I think no reasonable man will expect that, as human nature is constituted, the enormous influence of the crown should cease to prevail over the virtue of individuals. The mischief lies too deep to be cured by any remedy less.than some great convulsion, which may either carry back the constitution to its original principles, or utterly destroy it. I do not doubt that, in the first session after the next election, some popular measures may be adopted. The present house of commons have injured themselves by a too early and public profession of their principles; and if a strain of prostitution, which had no example, were within the reach of emulation, it might be imprudent to hazard the experiment too soon. But after all, sir, it is very immaterial whether a house of commons shall preserve their virtue for a week, a month, or a year. The influence which makes a septennial parliament dependent upon the pleasure of the crown, has a permanent operation, and cannot fail of success. My premises, I know, will be denied in argument, but every man's conscience tells him they are true. It remains then to be considered, whether it be for the interest of the people that privilege of parliament (which [z], in respect to the purposes for which it has hitherto been acquiesced under, is merely nominal) should be contracted within some certain limits, or whether the subject shall be left at the mercy of a power arbitrary upon the face of it, and notoriously under the direction of the crown.

I do not mean to decline the question of right. On the contrary, sir, I join issue with the advocates for privilege, and affirm, that, ' excepting the cases

[z] ' The necessity of securing the house of commons against the
' king's power, so that no interruption might be given either to the
' attendance of the members in parliament, or to the freedom of de-
' bate, was the foundation of parliamentary privilege; and we may
' observe, in all the addresses of new appointed speakers to the so-
' vereign, the utmost privilege they demand is liberty of speech and
' freedom from arrests. The very word privilege, means no more
' than immunity, or a safeguard to the party who possesses it, and
' can never be construed into an active power of invading the rights
' of others.'

'wherein the house of commons are a court of judicature (to which, from the nature of their office, a coercive power must belong), and excepting such contempts as immediately interrupt their proceedings, they have no legal authority to imprison any man for any supposed violation of privilege whatsoever.' It is not pretended that privilege, as now claimed, has ever been defined or confirmed by statute; neither can it be said, with any colour of truth, to be a part of the common law of England, which had grown into prescription long before we knew any thing of the existence of a house of commons. As for the law of parliament, it is only another name for the privilege in question; and since the power of creating new privileges has been formally renounced by both houses, since there is no code in which we can study the law of parliament, we have but one way left to make ourselves acquainted with it; that is, to compare the nature of the institution of a house of commons with the facts upon record. To establish a claim of privilege in either house, and to distinguish original right from usurpation, it must appear that it is indispensably necessary for the performance of the duty they are employed in, and also that it has been uniformly allowed. From the first part of this description it follows clearly, that whatever privilege does of right belong to the present house of commons, did equally belong to the first assembly of their predecessors, was as completely vested in them, and might have been exercised in the same extent. From the second we must infer that privileges which, for several centuries, were not only never allowed, but never even claimed, by the house of commons, must be founded upon usurpation. The constitutional duties of a house of commons are not very complicated nor mysterious. They are to propose or assent to wholesome laws for the benefit of the nation. They are to grant the necessary aids to the king, petition for the redress of grievances, and prosecute treason or high crimes against the state. If unlimited privilege be necessary to the performance of these duties, we have reason to conclude that, for many centuries after the institution of the house of commons, they were never performed. I am not bound to prove a negative, but I appeal to the English history when I affirm that, with the exceptions already stated (which yet I might safely relinquish), there is no precedent, from the year 1265 to the death of queen Elizabeth, of the house of commons having imprisoned any man (not a member of their house) for contempt or breach of privilege. In the most flagrant cases, and when their acknowledged privileges were most grossly violated, the poor commons, as they then styled themselves, never took the power of punishment into their own hands. They either sought redress by petition to the king, or, what is more remarkable, applied for justice to the house of lords; and when satisfaction was denied them or delayed, their only remedy was to refuse proceeding upon the king's business. So little conception had our ancestors of the monstrous doctrines now maintained concerning privilege, that in the reign of Elizabeth even liberty of speech, the vital principle of a deliberative assembly, was restrained, by the queen's authority, to a simple aye or no; and this restriction, though imposed upon three successive parliaments[a], was never once disputed by the house of commons.

I know there are many precedents of arbitrary commitments for contempt. But besides that they are of too modern a date to warrant a presumption that such a power was originally vested in the house of commons, fact alone does not constitute right. If it does, general warrants were lawful. An ordinance of the two houses has a force equal to law;

[a] In the years 1593, 1597, and 1601.

and the criminal jurisdiction assumed by the commons in 1621, in the case of Edward Lloyd, is a good precedent to warrant the like proceedings against any man who shall unadvisedly mention the folly of a king, or the ambition of a princess. The truth is, sir, that the greatest and most exceptionable part of the privileges now contended for, were introduced and asserted by a house of commons which abolished both monarchy and peerage, and whose proceedings, although they ended in one glorious act of substantial justice, could no way be reconciled to the forms of the constitution. Their successors profited by the example, and confirmed their power by a moderate or a popular use of it. Thus it grew by degrees, from a notorious innovation at one period, to be tacitly admitted as the privilege of parliament at another.

If, however, it could be proved, from considerations of necessity or convenience, that an unlimited power of commitment ought to be intrusted to the house of commons, and that in fact they have exercised it without opposition, still, in contemplation of law, the presumption is strongly against them. It is a leading maxim of the laws of England (and without it all laws are nugatory), that there is no right without a remedy, nor any legal power without a legal course to carry it into effect. Let the power now in question be tried by this rule. The speaker issues his warrant of attachment. The party attacked either resists force with force, or appeals to a magistrate, who declares the warrant illegal, and discharges the prisoner. Does the law provide no legal means for enforcing a legal warrant? Is there no regular proceeding pointed out in our law books to assert and vindicate the authority of so high a court as the house of commons? The question is answered directly by the fact. Their unlawful commands are resisted, and they have no remedy. The imprisonment of their own members is revenge indeed, but it is no assertion of the privilege they contend for [b]. Their whole proceeding stops, and there they stand, ashamed to retreat, and unable to advance. Sir, these ignorant men should be informed that the execution of the laws of England is not left in this uncertain, defenceless condition. If the process of the courts of Westminster-hall be resisted,

---

[b] Upon their own principles, they should have committed Mr. Wilkes, who had been guilty of a greater offence than even the lord mayor or alderman Oliver. But, after repeatedly ordering him to attend, they at last adjourned beyond the day appointed for his attendance, and by this mean, pitiful evasion gave up the point.

they have a direct course, sufficient to enforce submission. The court of king's bench commands the sheriff to raise the posse comitatus. The courts of chancery and exchequer issue a writ of rebellion, which must also be supported, if necessary, by the power of the county. To whom will our honest representatives direct their writ of rebellion? The guards, I doubt not, are willing enough to be employed, but they know nothing of the doctrine of writs, and may think it necessary to wait for a letter from lord Barrington.

It may now be objected to me, that my arguments prove too much; for that certainly there may be instances of contempt and insult to the house of commons, which do not fall within my own exceptions, yet, in regard to the dignity of the house, ought not to pass unpunished. Be it so. The courts of criminal jurisdiction are open to prosecutions, which the attorney general may commence by information or indictment. A libel, tending to asperse or vilify the house of commons, or any of their members, may be as severely punished in the court of king's bench, as a libel upon the king. Mr. De Grey thought so when he drew up the information of my letter to his majesty, or he had no meaning in charging it to be a scandalous libel upon the house of commons. In my opinion, they would consult their real dignity much better by appealing to the laws when they are offended, than by violating the first principle of natural justice, which forbids us to be judges when we are parties to the cause[c].

I do not mean to pursue them through the remainder of their proceedings. In their first resolutions it is possible they might have been deceived by ill-considered precedents. For the rest, there is no colour of palliation or excuse. They have advised the king to resume a power of dispensing with the laws by royal proclamation[d]; and kings we see are

[c] ' If it be demanded, in case a subject should be committed by
' either house for a matter manifestly out of their jurisdiction, what
' remedy can he have? I answer, that it cannot well be imagined
' that the law, which favours nothing more than the liberty of the
' subject, should give us a remedy against commitments by the king
' himself, appearing to be illegal, and yet give us no manner of redress against a commitment by our fellow subjects, equally appearing to be unwarranted. But as this is a case which, I am persuaded, will never happen, it seems needless over-nicely to examine
' it.'—Hawkins 2. 110.——N. B. He was a good lawyer, but no prophet.

[d] That their practice might be every way conformable to their principles, the house proceeded to advise the crown to publish a proclamation universally acknowledged to be illegal. Mr. Moreton publicly protested against it before it was issued; and lord Mansfield,

ready enough to follow such advice. By mere violence, and without the shadow of right, they have expunged the record of a judicial proceeding[e]. Nothing remained, but to attribute to their own vote a power of stopping the whole distribution of criminal and civil justice.

The public virtues of the chief magistrate have long since ceased to be in question. But it is said that he has private good qualities, and I myself have been ready to acknowledge them. They are now brought to the test. If he loves his people, he will dissolve a parliament which they can never confide in or respect. If he has any regard for his own honour, he will disdain to be any longer connected with such abandoned prostitution. But if it were conceivable, that a king of this country had lost all sense of personal honour, and all concern for the welfare of his subjects, I confess, sir, I should be

though not scrupulous to an extreme, speaks of it with horror. It is remarkable enough that the very men who advised the proclamation, and who hear it arraigned every day both within doors and without, are not daring enough to utter one word in its defence, nor have they ventured to take the least notice of Mr. Wilkes for discharging the persons apprehended under it.

[e] Lord Chatham very properly called this the act of a mob, not of a senate.

contented to renounce the forms of the constitution once more, if there were no other way to obtain substantial justice for the people'.

JUNIUS.

' When Mr. Wilkes was to be punished, they made no scruple about the privileges of parliament; and although it was as well known as any matter of public record and uninterrupted custom could be, ' that the members of either house are privileged except ' in case of treason, felony, or breach of peace,' they declared, without hesitation, ' that privilege of parliament did not extend to the ' case of a seditious libel;' and undoubtedly they would have done the same if Mr. Wilkes had been prosecuted for any other misdemeanor whatsoever. The ministry are of a sudden grown wonderfully careful of privileges, which their predecessors were as ready to invade. The known laws of the land, the rights of the subject, the sanctity of charters, and the reverence due to our magistrates, must all give way, without question or resistance, to a privilege of which no man knows either the origin or the extent. The house of commons judge of their own privileges without appeal: they may take offence at the most innocent action, and imprison the person who offends them during their arbitrary will and pleasure. The party has no remedy; he cannot appeal from their jurisdiction: and if he questions the privilege which he is supposed to have violated, it becomes an aggravation of his offence. Surely this doctrine is not to be found in Magna Charta. If it be admitted without limitation, I affirm that there is neither law nor liberty in this kingdom. We are the slaves of the house of commons, and, through them, we are the slaves of the king and his ministers. ANONYMOUS.

LETTER XLV.

TO

THE PRINTER OF THE PUBLIC ADVERTISER.

SIR,　　　　　　　　　　　1 May, 1771.

THEY who object to detached parts of Junius's last letter, either do not mean him fairly, or have not considered the general scope and course of his argument. There are degrees in all the private vices. Why not in public prostitution? The influence of the crown naturally makes a septennial parliament dependent. Does it follow that every house of commons will plunge at once into the lowest depth of prostitution? Junius supposes that the present house of commons, in going such enormous lengths, have been imprudent to themselves, as well as wicked to the public; that their example is not within the reach of emulation; and that, in the first session after the next election, some popular measures may probably be adopted. He does not expect that a dissolution of parliament will destroy corruption, but that at least it will be a check and terror to their successors, who will have seen that, in flagrant cases, their constituents can and will interpose with effect. After all, sir, will you not endeavour to remove or alleviate the most dangerous symptoms, because you cannot eradicate the disease? Will you not punish treason or parricide, because the sight of a gibbet does not prevent highway robberies? When the main argument of Junius is admitted to be answerable, I think it would become the minor critic, who hunts for blemishes, to be a little more distrustful of his own sagacity. The other objection is hardly worth an answer. When Junius observes that kings are ready enough to follow such advice, he does not mean to insinuate that, if the advice of parliament were good, the king would be so ready to follow it.

PHILO JUNIUS.

LETTER XLVI.

ADDRESSED TO

THE PRINTER OF THE PUBLIC ADVERTISER.

SIR, 22 May, 1771.

VERY early in the debate upon the decision of the Middlesex election, it was well observed by Junius, that the house of commons had not only exceeded their boasted precedent of the expulsion and subsequent incapacitation of Mr. Walpole, but that they had not even adhered to it strictly as far as it went. After convicting Mr. Dyson of giving a false quotation from the journals, and having explained the purpose which that contemptible fraud was intended to answer, he proceeds to state the vote itself by which Mr. Walpole's supposed incapacity was declared, viz. ' Resolved, That Robert
' Walpole, esq. having been this session of parlia-
' ment committed a prisoner to the tower, and ex-
' pelled this house for a high breach of trust in the

' execution of his office, and notorious corruption
' when secretary at war, was and is incapable of be-
' ing elected a member to serve in this present par-
' liament.' And then observes that, from the terms
of the vote, we have no right to annex the incapacitation to the expulsion only, for that, as the proposition stands, it must arise equally from the expulsion
and the commitment to the tower. I believe, sir,
no man who knows any thing of dialectics, or who
understands English, will dispute the truth and fair-
ness of this construction. But Junius has a great
authority to support him, which, to speak with the
duke of Grafton, I accidentally met with this morning in the course of my reading. It contains an admonition which cannot be repeated too often. Lord
Sommers, in his excellent tract upon the rights of
the people, after reciting the votes of the convention
of the 28th of January, 1689, viz. ' That king James
' the Second, having endeavoured to subvert the
' constitution of this kingdom, by breaking the ori-
' ginal contract between king and people; and by
' the advice of jesuits and other wicked persons hav-
' ing violated the fundamental laws, and having
' withdrawn himself out of this kingdom, hath ab-
' dicated the government, &c.' makes this observa-

tion upon it. ' The word abdicated relates to all
' the clauses aforegoing, as well as to his deserting
' the kingdom, or else they would have been wholly
' in vain.' And, that there might be no pretence
for confining the abdication merely to the withdrawing, lord Sommers farther observes, ' That king
' James, by refusing to govern us according to that
' law by which he held the crown, did implicitly
' renounce his title to it.'

If Junius's construction of the vote against Mr.
Walpole be now admitted (and indeed I cannot comprehend how it can honestly be disputed), the advocates of the house of commons must either give
up their precedent entirely, or be reduced to the necessity of maintaining one of the grossest absurdities
imaginable, viz. ' That a commitment to the tower
' is a constituent part of, and contributes half at
' least to the incapacitation of the person who suf-
' fers it.'

I need not make you any excuse for endeavouring to keep alive the attention of the public to the
decision of the Middlesex election. The more I
consider it, the more I am convinced that, as a

fact, it is indeed highly injurious to the rights of the people; but that, as a precedent, it is one of the most dangerous that ever was established against those who are to come after us. Yet I am so far a moderate man, that I verily believe the majority of the house of commons, when they passed this dangerous vote, neither understood the question, nor knew the consequence of what they were doing. Their motives were rather despicable than criminal in the extreme. One effect they certainly did not foresee. They are now reduced to such a situation, that if a member of the present house of commons were to conduct himself ever so improperly, and in reality deserve to be sent back to his constituents with a mark of disgrace, they would not dare to expel him, because they know that the people, in order to try again the great question of right, or to thwart an odious house of commons, would probably overlook his immediate unworthiness, and return the same person to parliament. But in time the precedent will gain strength. A future house of commons will have no such apprehensions, consequently will not scruple to follow a precedent which they did not establish. The miser himself seldom lives to enjoy the fruit of his extortion; but his heir succeeds to him of course, and takes possession without censure. No man expects him to make restitution, and no matter for his title, he lives quietly upon the estate.

PHILO JUNIUS.

LETTER XLVII.

TO

THE PRINTER OF THE PUBLIC ADVERTISER.

SIR, 25 May, 1771.

I CONFESS my partiality to Junius, and feel a considerable pleasure in being able to communicate any thing to the public in support of his opinions. The doctrine laid down in his last letter, concerning the power of the house of commons to commit for contempt, is not so new as it appeared to many people, who, dazzled with the name of privilege, had never suffered themselves to examine the question fairly. In the course of my reading this morning, I met with the following passage in the journals of the house of commons. (Vol. I. p. 603.) Upon occasion of a jurisdiction unlawfully assumed by the house in the year 1621, Mr. Attorney general Noye gave his opinion as follows. ' No doubt but,
' in some cases, this house may give judgment;—
' in matters of returns, and concerning members of

' our house, or falling out in our view in parlia-
' ment; but, for foreign matters, knoweth not how
' we can judge it. Knoweth not that we have been
' used to give judgment in any case but those before
' mentioned.'

Sir Edward Coke, upon the same subject, says (page 604), ' No question but this is a house of re-
' cord, and that it hath power of judicature in some
' cases—have power to judge of returns and mem-
' bers of our house; one, no member, offending out
' of the parliament, when he came hither and justi-
' fied it, was censured for it.'

Now, sir, if you will compare the opinion of these great sages of the law with Junius's doctrine, you will find they tally exactly. He allows the power of the house to commit their own members (which however they may grossly abuse). He allows their power in cases where they are acting as a court of judicature, viz. elections, returns, &c. and he allows it in such contempts as immediately interrupt their proceedings, or, as Mr. Noye expresses it, ' falling out in their view in parliament.'

They who would carry the privileges of parliament farther than Junius, either do not mean well to the public, or know not what they are doing. The government of England is a government of law. We betray ourselves, we contradict the spirit of our laws, and we shake the whole system of English jurisprudence, whenever we intrust a discretionary power over the life, liberty, or fortune, of the subject, to any man, or set of men whatsoever, upon a presumption that it will not be abused.

PHILO JUNIUS.

LETTER XLVIII.

TO

THE PRINTER OF THE PUBLIC ADVERTISER.

SIR,   28 May, 1771.

Any man, who takes the trouble of perusing the journals of the house of commons, will soon be convinced, that very little, if any, regard at all ought to be paid to the resolutions of one branch of the legislature, declaratory of the law of the land, or even of what they call the law of parliament. It will appear that these resolutions have no one of the properties by which, in this country particularly, law is distinguished from mere will and pleasure; but that, on the contrary, they bear every mark of a power arbitrarily assumed and capriciously applied:—That they are usually made in times of contest, and to serve some unworthy purpose of passion or party;—that the law is seldom declared until after the fact, by which it is supposed to be violated;—that legislation and jurisdiction are united in the

same persons, and exercised at the same moment;—
and that a court, from which there is no appeal, assumes an original jurisdiction in a criminal case;—
in short, sir, to collect a thousand absurdities into
one mass, ' we have a law which cannot be known
' because it is ex post facto, the party is both legi-
' slator and judge, and the jurisdiction is without
' appeal.' Well might the judges say, The law of
parliament is above us.

You will not wonder, sir, that, with these qualifications, the declaratory resolutions of the house
of commons should appear to be in perpetual contradiction, not only to common sense and to the
laws we are acquainted with (and which alone we
can obey), but even to one another. I was led to
trouble you with these observations by a passage
which, to speak in lutestring, I met with this morning in the course of my reading, and upon which I
mean to put a question to the advocates for privilege.
On the 8th of March, 1704, (vide Journals, Vol. XIV.
p. 565) the house thought proper to come to the
following resolutions. 1. ' That no commoner of
' England, committed by the house of commons for
' breach of privilege or contempt of that house,
' ought to be, by any writ of habeas corpus, made

' to appear in any other place, or before any other
' judicature, during that session of parliament where-
' in such person was so committed.'

2. ' That the serjeant at arms attending this house
' do make no return of, or yield any obedience to,
' the said writs of habeas corpus, and for such his
' refusal, that he have the protection of the house
' of commons [g].'

Welbore Ellis, What say you? Is this the law of parliament, or is it not? I am a plain man, sir, and cannot follow you through the phlegmatic forms of an oration. Speak out, Grildrig; say yes, or no. If you say yes, I shall then inquire by what authority Mr. de Grey, the honest lord Mansfield, and the barons of the exchequer, dared to grant a writ of

[g] If there be in reality any such law in England as the law of parliament, which (under the exceptions stated in my letter on privilege), I confess, after long deliberation, I very much doubt, it certainly is not constituted by, nor can it be collected from, the resolutions of either house, whether enacting or declaratory. I desire the reader will compare the above resolution of the year 1704, with the following of the 3d of April, 1628.—' Resolved, That the writ
' of habeas corpus cannot be denied, but ought to be granted to
' every man that is committed or detained in prison, or otherwise
' restrained, by the command of the king, the privy council, or
' any other, he praying the same.'

habeas corpus for bringing the bodies of the lord mayor and Mr. Oliver before them, and why the lieutenant of the tower made any return to a writ which the house of commons had in a similar instance declared to be unlawful. If you say no, take care you do not at once give up the cause, in support of which you have so long and so laboriously tortured your understanding. Take care you do not confess that there is no test by which we can distinguish, no evidence by which we can determine what is, and what is not, the law of parliament. The resolutions I have quoted stand upon your journals, uncontroverted and unrepealed; they contain a declaration of the law of parliament by a court competent to the question, and whose decision, as you and lord Mansfield say, must be law, because there is no appeal from it; and they were made not hastily, but after long deliberation upon a constitutional question. What farther sanction or solemnity will you annex to any resolution of the present house of commons, beyond what appears upon the face of those two resolutions, the legality of which you now deny? If you say that parliaments are not infallible, and that queen Anne, in consequence of the violent proceedings of that house of commons, was obliged to prorogue and dissolve them, I shall agree with you very heartily, and think that the precedent ought to be followed immediately. But you, Mr. Ellis, who hold this language, are inconsistent with your own principles. You have hitherto maintained that the house of commons are the sole judges of their own privileges, and that their declaration does, ipso facto, constitute the law of parliament; yet now you confess that parliaments are fallible, and that their resolutions may be illegal, consequently that their resolutions do not constitute the law of parliament. When the king was urged to dissolve the present parliament, you advised him to tell his subjects, that he was careful not to assume any of those powers which the constitution had placed in other hands, &c. Yet queen Anne, it seems, was justified in exerting her prerogative to stop a house of commons whose proceedings, compared with those of the assembly of which you are a most worthy member, were the perfection of justice and reason.

In what a labyrinth of nonsense does a man involve himself who labours to maintain falsehood by argument! How much better would it become the dignity of the house of commons to speak plainly to the people, and tell us at once, that their will must be obeyed, not because it is lawful and reasonable, but because it is their will. Their constituents would have a better opinion of their candour, and, I promise you, not a worse opinion of their integrity.

PHILO JUNIUS.

LETTER XLIX.

TO

HIS GRACE THE DUKE OF GRAFTON.

MY LORD,   22 June, 1771.

THE profound respect I bear to the gracious prince who governs this country with no less honour to himself than satisfaction to his subjects, and who restores you to your rank under his standard, will save you from a multitude of reproaches. The attention I should have paid to your failings is involuntarily attracted to the hand that rewards them; and though I am not so partial to the royal judgment, as to affirm, that the favour of a king can remove mountains of infamy, it serves to lessen at least, for undoubtedly it divides the burthen. While I remember how much is due to his sacred character, I cannot, with any decent appearance of propriety, call you the meanest and the basest fellow in the kingdom. I protest, my lord, I do not think you so. You will have a dangerous rival in that kind of fame to which you have hitherto so happily directed your ambition, as long as there is one man living who thinks you worthy of his confidence, and fit to be trusted with any share in his government. I confess you have great intrinsic merit; but take care you do not value it too highly. Consider how much of it would have been lost to the world, if the king had not graciously affixed his stamp, and given it currency among his subjects. If it be true that a virtuous man, struggling with adversity, be a scene worthy of the gods, the glorious contention between you and the best of princes deserves a circle equally attentive and respectable. I think I already see other gods rising from the earth to behold it.

But this language is too mild for the occasion. The king is determined that our abilities shall not be lost to society. The perpetration and description of new crimes will find employment for us both.

My lord, if the persons who have been loudest in their professions of patriotism had done their duty to the public with the same zeal and perseverance that I did, I will not assert that government would have recovered its dignity, but at least our gracious sovereign must have spared his subjects this last insult[h], which, if there be any feeling left among us, they will resent more than even the real injuries they received from every measure of your grace's administration. In vain would he have looked round him for another character so consummate as yours. Lord Mansfield shrinks from his principles; his ideas of government perhaps go farther than your own, but his heart disgraces the theory of his understanding. Charles Fox is yet in blossom; and as for Mr. Wedderburne, there is something about him which even treachery cannot trust. For the present, therefore, the best of princes must have contented himself with lord Sandwich. You would long since have received your final dismission and reward; and I, my lord, who do not esteem you the more for the high office you possess, would willingly have followed you to your retirement. There is surely something singularly benevolent in the character of our sovereign. From the moment he ascended the throne, there is

[h] The duke was lately appointed lord privy seal.

no crime, of which human nature is capable (and I call upon the recorder to witness it), that has not appeared venial in his sight. With any other prince, the shameful desertion of him, in the midst of that distress which you alone had created, in the very crisis of danger, when he fancied he saw the throne already surrounded by men of virtue and abilities, would have outweighed the memory of your former services. But his majesty is full of justice, and understands the doctrine of compensations. He remembers with gratitude how soon you had accommodated your morals to the necessity of his service; how cheerfully had you abandoned the engagements of private friendship, and renounced the most solemn professions to the public. The sacrifice of lord Chatham was not lost upon him. Even the cowardice and perfidy of deserting him may have done you no disservice in his esteem. The instance was painful, but the principle might please.

You did not neglect the magistrate while you flattered the man. The expulsion of Mr. Wilkes predetermined in the cabinet; the power of depriving the subject of his birthright, attributed to a resolution of one branch of the legislature; the constitution impudently invaded by the house of commons; the right of defending it treacherously re-nounced by the house of lords. These are the strokes, my lord, which, in the present reign, recommend to office, and constitute a minister. They would have determined your sovereign's judgment if they had made no impression upon his heart. We need not look for any other species of merit to account for his taking the earliest opportunity to recall you to his councils. Yet you have other merit in abundance. Mr. Hine, the duke of Portland, and Mr. Yorke. Breach of trust, robbery, and murder. You would think it a compliment to your gallantry, if I added rape to the catalogue; but the style of your amours secures you from resistance. I know how well these several charges have been defended. In the first instance, the breach of trust is supposed to have been its own reward. Mr. Bradshaw affirms upon his honour (and so may the gift of smiling never depart from him), that you reserved no part of Mr. Hine's purchase-money for your own use, but that every shilling of it was scrupulously paid to governor Burgoyne. Make haste, my lord; another patent, applied in time, may keep the [1] Oaks

---

[1] A superb villa of colonel Burgoyne, about this time advertised for sale.

in the family. If not, Birnham wood, I fear, must come to the Macaroni.

The duke of Portland was in life your earliest friend. In defence of his property he had nothing to plead but equity against sir James Lowther, and prescription against the crown. You felt for your friend; but the law must take its course. Posterity will scarce believe that lord Bute's son in law had barely interest enough at the treasury to get his grant completed before the general election[k].

Enough has been said of that detestable transaction which ended in the death of Mr. Yorke. I cannot speak of it without horror and compassion. To excuse yourself, you publicly impeach your accomplice, and to his mind perhaps the accusation may be flattery. But in murder you are both principals. It was once a question of emulation, and if the event had not disappointed the immediate schemes of the closet, it might still have been a hopeful subject of jest and merriment between you.

[k] It will appear by a subsequent letter, that the duke's precipitation proved fatal to the grant. It looks like the hurry and confusion of a young highwayman, who takes a few shillings, but leaves the purse and watch behind him. And yet the duke was an old offender!

This letter, my lord, is only a preface to my future correspondence. The remainder of the summer shall be dedicated to your amusement. I mean now and then to relieve the severity of your morning studies, and to prepare you for the business of the day. Without pretending to more than Mr. Bradshaw's sincerity, you may rely upon my attachment as long as you are in office.

Will your grace forgive me, if I venture to express some anxiety for a man whom I know you do not love? My lord Weymouth has cowardice to plead, and a desertion of a later date than your own. You know the privy seal was intended for him; and if you consider the dignity of the post he deserted, you will hardly think it decent to quarter him on Mr. Rigby. Yet he must have bread, my lord; or rather he must have wine. If you deny him the cup, there will be no keeping him within the pale of the ministry.

JUNIUS.

LETTER L.

TO

HIS GRACE THE DUKE OF GRAFTON.

MY LORD, 9 June, 1771.

THE influence of your grace's fortune still seems to preside over the treasury. The genius of Mr. Bradshaw inspires Mr. Robinson [1]. How remarkable it is (and I speak of it not as matter of reproach, but as something peculiar to your character) that you have never yet formed a friendship which has not been fatal to the object of it, nor

---

[1] By an intercepted letter from the secretary of the treasury it appeared that the friends of government were to be very active in supporting the ministerial nomination of sheriffs.

adopted a cause to which, one way or other, you have not done mischief. Your attachment is infamy while it lasts, and, whichever way it turns, leaves ruin and disgrace behind it. The deluded girl who yields to such a profligate, even while he is constant, forfeits her reputation as well as her innocence, and finds herself abandoned at last to misery and shame. Thus it happened with the best of princes. Poor Dingley too! I protest I hardly know which of them we ought most to lament—The unhappy man who sinks under the sense of his dishonour, or him who survives it. Characters, so finished, are placed beyond the reach of panegyric. Death has fixed his seal upon Dingley, and you, my lord, have set your mark upon the other.

The only letter I ever addressed to the king was so unkindly received, that I believe I shall never presume to trouble his majesty in that way again. But my zeal for his service is superior to neglect, and, like Mr. Wilkes's patriotism, thrives by persecution. Yet his majesty is much addicted to useful reading, and, if I am not ill-informed, has honoured the Public Advertiser with particular attention. I have endeavoured therefore, and not without success (as perhaps you may remember), to furnish it with such

Lord Bute

interesting and edifying intelligence, as probably would not reach him through any other channel. The services you have done the nation, your integrity in office, and signal fidelity to your approved good master, have been faithfully recorded. Nor have his own virtues been entirely neglected. These letters, my lord, are read in other countries and in other languages; and I think I may affirm without vanity, that the gracious character of the best of princes is by this time not only perfectly known to his subjects, but tolerably well understood by the rest of Europe. In this respect alone I have the advantage of Mr. Whitehead. His plan, I think, is too narrow. He seems to manufacture his verses for the sole use of the hero who is supposed to be the subject of them, and, that his meaning may not be exported in foreign bottoms, sets all translation at defiance.

Your grace's re-appointment to a seat in the cabinet was announced to the public by the ominous return of lord Bute to this country. When that noxious planet approaches England, he never fails to bring plague and pestilence along with him. The king already feels the malignant effect of your influence over his councils. Your former administration made Mr. Wilkes an alderman of London, and representative of Middlesex. Your next appearance in office is marked with his election to the shrievalty. In whatever measure you are concerned, you are not only disappointed of success, but always contrive to make the government of the best of princes contemptible in his own eyes, and ridiculous to the whole world. Making all due allowance for the effect of the minister's declared interposition, Mr. Robinson's activity, and Mr. Horne's new zeal in support of administration, we still want the genius of the duke of Grafton to account for committing the whole interest of government in the city to the conduct of Mr. Harley. I will not bear hard upon your faithful friend and emissary Mr. Touchet, for I know the difficulties of his situation, and that a few lottery tickets are of use to his economy. There is a proverb concerning persons in the predicament of this gentleman, which however cannot be strictly applied to him. They commence dupes, and finish knaves. Now Mr. Touchet's character is uniform. I am convinced that his sentiments never depended upon his circumstances, and that, in the most prosperous state of his fortune, he was always the very man he is at present. But was there no other person of rank and consequence in the city, whom government could confide in, but a notorious jacobite? Did you imagine that the whole body of the dissenters, that the whole whig-interest of London, would attend at the levee, and submit to the directions of a notorious jacobite? Was there no whig magistrate in the city to whom the servants of George the Third could intrust the management of a business so very interesting to their master as the election of sheriffs? Is there no room at St. James's but for Scotchmen and jacobites? My lord, I do not mean to question the sincerity of Mr. Harley's attachment to his majesty's government. Since the commencement of the present reign I have seen still greater contradictions reconciled. The principles of these worthy jacobites are not so absurd as they have been represented. Their ideas of divine right are not so much annexed to the person or family, as to the political character of the sovereign. Had there ever been an honest man among the Stuarts, his majesty's present friends would have been whigs upon principle. But the conversion of the best of princes has removed their scruples. They have forgiven him the sins of his Hanoverian ancestors, and acknowledge the hand of Providence in the descent of the crown upon the head of a true Stuart. In you, my lord, they also behold, with a kind of predilection which borders upon loyalty, the natural representative of that illustrious family. The mode of your descent from Charles the Second is only a bar to your pretensions to the crown, and no way interrupts the regularity of your succession to all the virtues of the Stuarts.

The unfortunate success of the reverend Mr. Horne's endeavours in support of the ministerial nomination of sheriffs, will I fear obstruct his preferment. Permit me to recommend him to your grace's protection. You will find him copiously gifted with those qualities of the heart which usually direct you in the choice of your friendships. He too was Mr. Wilkes's friend, and as incapable as you are of the liberal resentment of a gentleman. No, my lord, it was the solitary, vindictive malice of a monk, brooding over the infirmities of his friend, until he thought they quickened into public life, and feasting, with a rancorous rapture, upon the sordid catalogue of his distresses. Now, let him go back to his cloister. The church is a proper retreat for him. In his principles he is already a bishop.

The mention of this man has moved me from my natural moderation. Let me return to your grace. You are the pillow upon which I am determined to rest all my resentments. What idea can the best of sovereigns form to himself of his own government? in what repute can he conceive that he stands with his people, when he sees, beyond the possibility of a doubt, that, whatever be the office, the suspicion of his favour is fatal to the candidate, and that, when the party he wishes well to has the fairest prospect of success, if his royal inclination should unfortunately be discovered, it drops like an acid, and turns the election? This event, among others, may perhaps contribute to open his majesty's eyes to his real honour and interest. In spite of all your grace's ingenuity, he may at last perceive the inconvenience of selecting, with such a curious felicity, every villain in the nation to fill the various departments of his government. Yet I should be sorry to confine him in the choice either of his footmen or his friends.

JUNIUS.

LETTER LI.

FROM

THE REVEREND MR. HORNE TO JUNIUS.

SIR, 13 July, 1771.

FARCE, comedy, and tragedy,—Wilkes, Foote, and Junius, united at the same time against one poor parson, are fearful odds. The two former are only labouring in their vocation, and may equally plead in excuse, that their aim is a livelihood. I admit the plea for the second; his is an honest calling, and my clothes were lawful game; but I cannot so readily approve Mr. Wilkes, or commend him for making patriotism a trade, and a fraudulent trade. But what shall I say to Junius? the grave, the solemn, the didactic! Ridicule, indeed, has been ridiculously called the test of truth; but surely to confess that you lose your natural moderation when mention is made of the man, does not promise much truth or justice when you speak of him yourself.

You charge me with ' a new zeal in support of
' administration,' and with ' endeavours in support
' of the ministerial nomination of sheriffs.' The reputation which your talents have deservedly gained
to the signature of Junius, draws from me a reply,
which I disdained to give to the anonymous lies of
Mr. Wilkes. You make frequent use of the word
gentleman; I only call myself a man, and desire no
other distinction: if you are either, you are bound
to make good your charges, or to confess that you
have done me a hasty injustice upon no authority.

I put the matter fairly to issue.—I say, that so
far from any new ' zeal in support of administra-
' tion,' I am possessed with the utmost abhorrence
of their measures; and that I have ever shewn myself, and am still ready, in any rational manner, to
lay down all I have—my life, in opposition to those
measures. I say, that I have not, and never have
had, any communication or connexion of any kind,
directly or indirectly, with any courtier or ministerial man, or any of their adherents: that I never
have received, or solicited, or expected, or desired,
or do now hope for, any reward of any sort, from
any party or set of men in administration or opposition; I say, that I never used any ' endeavours in

' support of the ministerial nomination of sheriffs:' that I did not solicit any one liveryman for his vote for any one of the candidates, nor employ any other person to solicit: and that I did not write one single line or word in favour of Messrs. Plumbe and Kirkman, whom I understand to have been supported by the ministry.—

You are bound to refute what I here advance, or to lose your credit for veracity. You must produce facts; surmise and general abuse, in however elegant language, ought not to pass for proofs. You have every advantage, and I have every disadvantage: you are unknown, I give my name: all parties, both in and out of administration, have their reasons (which I shall relate hereafter) for uniting in their wishes against me: and the popular prejudice is as strongly in your favour, as it is violent against the parson.

Singular as my present situation is, it is neither painful, nor was it unforeseen. He is not fit for public business who does not even at his entrance prepare his mind for such an event. Health, fortune, tranquillity, and private connexions, I have sacrificed upon the altar of the public; and the only return I receive, because I will not concur to dupe and mislead a senseless multitude, is barely, that they have not yet torn me in pieces. That this has been the only return, is my pride, and a source of more real satisfaction than honours or prosperity. I can practise, before I am old, the lessons I learned in my youth; nor shall I ever forget the words of my ancient monitor:

'Tis the last key-stone
'That makes the arch: the rest that there were put,
'Are nothing till that comes to bind and shut.
'Then stands it a triumphal mark! then men
'Observe the strength, the height, the why and when
'It was erected; and still walking under,
'Meet some new matter to look up and wonder!'

I am, sir, your humble servant,

JOHN HORNE.

LETTER LII.

TO
THE REVEREND MR. HORNE.

SIR,   24 July, 1771.

    I CANNOT descend to an altercation with you in the newspapers. But since I have attacked your character, and you complain of injustice, I think you have some right to an explanation. You defy me to prove that you solicited a vote, or wrote a word in support of the ministerial alderman. Sir, I did never suspect you of such folly. It would have been impossible for Mr. Horne to have solicited votes, or to have written for the newspapers in defence of that cause, without being detected and brought to shame. Neither do I pretend to any intelligence concerning you, or to know more of your conduct, than you yourself have thought proper to communicate to the public. It is from your own letters I conclude that you have sold yourself to the ministry; or, if that charge be too

W. Ridley sculp.

John Horne Tooke Esq.

severe, and supposing it possible to be deceived by appearances so very strongly against you, what are your friends to say in your defence? Must they not confess that, to gratify your personal hatred of Mr. Wilkes, you sacrificed, as far as depended upon your interest and abilities, the cause of the country? I can make allowance for the violence of the passions; and if ever I should be convinced that you had no motive but to destroy Wilkes, I shall then be ready to do justice to your character, and to declare to the world, that I despise you somewhat less than I do at present. But as a public man I must for ever condemn you. You cannot but know,—nay, you dare not pretend to be ignorant, that the highest gratification of which the most detestable in this nation is capable, would have been the defeat of Wilkes. I know that man much better than any of you. Nature intended him only for a good-humoured fool. A systematical education, with long practice, has made him a consummate hypocrite. Yet this man, to say nothing of his worthy ministers, you have most assiduously laboured to gratify. To exclude Wilkes, it was not necessary you should solicit votes for his opponents. We incline the balance as effectually by lessening the weight in one scale, as by increasing it in the other.

The mode of your attack upon Wilkes (though I am far from thinking meanly of your abilities) convinces me, that you either want judgment extremely, or that you are blinded by your resentment. You ought to have foreseen that the charges you urged against Wilkes could never do him any mischief. After all, when we expected discoveries highly interesting to the community, what a pitiful detail did it end in!—Some old clothes, a Welch poney, a French footman, and a hamper of claret. Indeed, Mr. Horne, the public should, and will forgive him his claret and his footmen, and even the ambition of making his brother chamberlain of London, as long as he stands forth against a ministry and parliament who are doing every thing they can to enslave the country, and as long as he is a thorn in the king's side. You will not suspect me of setting up Wilkes for a perfect character. The question to the public is, Where shall we find a man who, with purer principles, will go the lengths, and run the hazards, that he has done? The season calls for such a man, and he ought to be supported. What would have been the triumph of that odious hypocrite and his minions, if Wilkes had been defeated! It was not your fault, reverend sir, that he did not enjoy it completely. But now, I promise you, you have so little power to do mischief, that I much question whether the ministry will adhere to the promises they have made you. It will be in vain to say that I am a partizan of Mr. Wilkes, or personally your enemy. You will convince no man, for you do not believe it yourself. Yet, I confess, I am a little offended at the low rate at which you seem to value my understanding. I beg, Mr. Horne, you will hereafter believe that I measure the integrity of men by their conduct, not by their professions. Such tales may entertain Mr. Oliver, or your grandmother, but, trust me, they are thrown away upon Junius.

You say you are a man. Was it generous, was it manly, repeatedly to introduce into a newspaper the name of a young lady with whom you must heretofore have lived on terms of politeness and good-humour? But I have done with you. In my opinion your credit is irrecoverably ruined. Mr. Townsend, I think, is nearly in the same predicament. Poor Oliver has been shamefully duped by you. You have made him sacrifice all the honour he got by his imprisonment. As for Mr. Sawbridge, whose character I really respect, I am astonished he does not see through your duplicity. Never was so base a design so poorly conducted. This letter, you see, is not intended for the public, but if you think it will do you any service, you are at liberty to publish it[m].

JUNIUS.

[m] This letter was transmitted privately by the printer to Mr. Horne, by Junius's request. Mr. Horne returned it to the printer, with directions to publish it.

LETTER LIII.

FROM

THE REVEREND MR. HORNE TO JUNIUS.

SIR, 31 July, 1771.

You have disappointed me. When I told you that surmise and general abuse, in however elegant language, ought not to pass for proofs, I evidently hinted at the reply which I expected: but you have dropped your usual elegance, and seem willing to try what will be the effect of surmise and general abuse in very coarse language. Your answer to my letter (which I hope was cool and temperate and modest) has convinced me that my idea of a man is much superior to yours of a gentleman. Of your former letters I have always said materiem superabat opus: I do not think so of the present; the principles are more detestable than the expressions are mean and iliberal. I am contented that all those who adopt the one should for ever load me with the other.

I appeal to the common sense of the public, to which I have ever directed myself. I believe they have it, though I am sometimes half-inclined to suspect that Mr. Wilkes has formed a truer judgment of mankind than I have. However of this I am sure, that there is nothing else upon which to place a steady reliance. Trick, and low cunning, and addressing their prejudices and passions, may be the fittest means to carry a particular point; but if they have not common sense, there is no prospect of gaining for them any real permanent good. The same passions which have been artfully used by an honest man for their advantage, may be more artfully employed by a dishonest man for their destruction. I desire them to apply their common sense to this letter of Junius, not for my sake, but their own; it concerns them most nearly, for the principles it contains lead to disgrace and ruin, and are inconsistent with every notion of civil society.

The charges which Junius has brought against me are made ridiculous by his own inconsistency and self-contradiction. He charges me positively with ' a new zeal in support of administration;' and with ' endeavours in support of the ministerial nomina-' tion of sheriffs.' And he assigns two inconsistent

motives for my conduct: either that I have ' sold
' myself to the ministry;' or am instigated ' by the
' solitary, vindictive malice of a monk:' either that
I am influenced by a sordid desire of gain; or am
hurried on by ' personal hatred, and blinded by re-
' sentment.' In his letter to the duke of Grafton
he supposes me actuated by both; in his letter to
me he at first doubts which of the two, whether interest, or revenge, is my motive: however, at last he
determines for the former, and again positively asserts that ' the ministry have made me promises;'
yet he produces no instance of corruption, nor pre-
tends to have any intelligence of a ministerial connexion: he mentions no cause of personal hatred to
Mr. Wilkes, nor any reason for my resentment, or
revenge; nor has Mr. Wilkes himself ever hinted
any, though repeatedly pressed. When Junius is
called upon to justify his accusation, he answers
' he cannot descend to an altercation with me in
' the newspapers.' Junius, who exists only in the
newspapers, who acknowledges ' he has attacked my
' character' there, and ' thinks I have some right
' to an explanation;' yet this Junius ' cannot de-
' scend to an altercation in the newspapers!' and
because he cannot descend to an altercation with me
in the newspapers, he sends a letter of abuse by the

printer, which he finishes with telling me ' I am at
' liberty to publish it.' This, to be sure, is a most
excellent method to avoid an altercation in the newspapers!

The proofs of his positive charges are as extraordinary. ' He does not pretend to any intelligence
' concerning me, or to know more of my conduct
' than I myself have thought proper to communi-
' cate to the public.' He does not suspect me of
such gross folly as to have solicited votes, or to have
written anonymously in the newspapers, because it
is impossible to do either of these without being detected and brought to shame. Junius says this! who
yet imagines that he has himself written two years
under that signature (and more under others), without being detected! his warmest admirers will not
hereafter add, without being brought to shame. But
though he did never suspect me of such gross folly
as to run the hazard of being detected and brought
to shame by anonymous writing, he insists that I
have been guilty of a much grosser folly, of incuring the certainty of shame and detection by writings
signed with my name! But this is a small flight
for the towering Junius: ' He is far from thinking
' meanly of my abilities,' though he is ' convinced

'that I want judgment extremely,' and can 'really
'respect Mr. Sawbridge's character,' though he declares him[n] to be so poor a creature as not to 'see
'through the basest design conducted in the poorest
'manner!' And this most base design is conducted
in the poorest manner by a man whom he does not
suspect of gross folly, and of whose abilities he is far
from thinking meanly!

Should we ask Junius to reconcile these contradictions, and explain this nonsense, the answer is
ready, ' he cannot descend to an altercation in the
' newspapers.' He feels no reluctance to attack the
character of any man: the throne is not too high,

[n] I beg leave to introduce Mr. Horne to the character of the
Double Dealer. I thought they had been better acquainted. 'An-
' other very wrong objection has been made by some who have not
' taken leisure to distinguish the character. The hero of the play
' (meaning Mellefont) is a gull, and made a fool, and cheated. Is
' every man a gull and a fool that is deceived? At that rate, I am
' afraid the two classes of men will be reduced to one, and the
' knaves themselves be at a loss to justify their title. But if an open,
' honest hearted man, who has an entire confidence in one whom
' he takes to be his friend, and who (to confirm him in his opinion)
' in all appearance and upon several trials has been so; if this man
' be deceived by the treachery of the other, must he of necessity
' commence fool immediately, only because the other has proved a
' villain?'—Yes, says parson Horne. No, says Congreve; and he,
I think, is allowed to have known something of human nature.

nor the cottage too low: his mighty malice can grasp both extremes: he hints not his accusations as opinion, conjecture, or inference; but delivers them as positive assertions. Do the accused complain of injustice? He acknowledges they have some sort of right to an explanation; but if they ask for proofs and facts, he begs to be excused: and, though he is no where else to be encountered, ' he cannot de-
' scend to an altercation in the newspapers.'

And this perhaps Junius may think ' the liberal
' resentment of a gentleman:' this skulking assassination he may call courage. In all things as in this I hope we differ:

> ' I thought that fortitude had been a mean
> ' 'Twixt fear and rashness; not a lust obscene
> ' Or appetite of offending; but a skill
> ' And nice discernment between good and ill.
> ' Her ends are honesty and public good,
> ' And without these she is not understood.'

Of two things however he has condescended to give proof. He very properly produces a young lady to prove that I am not a man: and a good old woman, my grandmother, to prove Mr. Oliver a fool. Poor old soul! she read her bible far otherwise than Junius! she often found there that the sins of the fathers had been visited on the children; and therefore was cautious that herself and her immediate descendants should leave no reproach on her posterity: and they left none. How little could she foresee this reverse of Junius, who visits my political sins upon my grandmother! I do not charge this to the score of malice in him, it proceeded entirely from his propensity to blunder; that whilst he was reproaching me for introducing, in the most harmless manner, the name of one female, he might himself, at the same instant, introduce two.

I am represented alternately, as it suits Junius's purpose, under the opposite characters of a gloomy monk, and a man of politeness and good-humour. I am called ' a solitary monk,' in order to confirm the notion given of me in Mr. Wilkes's anonymous paragraphs, that I never laugh: and the terms of politeness and good humour, on which I am said to have lived heretofore with the young lady, are intended to confirm other paragraphs of Mr. Wilkes, in which he is supposed to have offended me by refusing his daughter. Ridiculous! Yet I cannot deny but that Junius has proved me unmanly and ungenerous as clearly as he has shewn me corrupt and vindictive: and I will tell him more; I have paid the present ministry as many visits and compliments as ever I paid to the young lady, and shall all my life treat them with the same politeness and good-humour.

But Junius ' begs me to believe that he measures ' the integrity of men by their conduct, not by their ' professions.' Sure this Junius must imagine his readers as void of understanding as he is of modesty! Where shall we find the standard of his integrity? By what are we to measure the conduct of this lurking assassin? And he says this to me, whose conduct, wherever I could personally appear, has been as direct and open and public as my words; I have not, like him, concealed myself in my chamber to shoot my arrows out of the window; nor contented myself to view the battle from afar; but publicly mixed in the engagement, and shared the danger. To whom have I, like him, refused my name upon complaint of injury? what printer have I desired to conceal me? in the infinite variety of business I have been concerned, where it is not so easy to be faultless, which of my actions can he arraign? to what danger has any man been exposed which I have not faced? information, action, imprisonment, or death? what labour have I refused? what expence have I declined? what pleasure have I not

renounced? But Junius, to whom no conduct belongs, ' measures the integrity of men by their con-
' duct, not by their professions;' himself all the while being nothing but professions, and those too anonymous! The political ignorance or wilful falsehood of this declaimer is extreme: his own former letters justify both my conduct and those whom his last letter abuses: for the public measures which Junius has been all along defending, were ours, whom he attacks; and the uniform opposer of those measures has been Mr. Wilkes, whose bad actions and intentions he endeavours to screen.

Let Junius now, if he pleases, change his abuse; and, quitting his loose hold of interest and revenge, accuse me of vanity, and call this defence boasting. I own I have a pride to see statues decreed, and the highest honours conferred, for measures and actions which all men have approved: whilst those who counselled and caused them are execrated and insulted. The darkness in which Junius thinks himself shrouded, has not concealed him; nor the artifice of only attacking under that signature those he would pull down (whilst he recommends by other ways those he would have promoted) disguised from me whose partizan he is. When lord Chatham can forgive the awkward situation in which for the sake of the public he was designedly placed by the thanks to him from the city; and when Wilkes's name ceases to be necessary to lord Rockingham to keep up a clamour against the persons of the ministry, without obliging the different factions now in opposition to bind themselves beforehand to some certain points, and to stipulate some precise advantages to the public: then, and not till then, may those whom he now abuses expect the approbation of Junius. The approbation of the public for our faithful attention to their interests by endeavours for those stipulations which have made us as obnoxious to the factions in opposition as to those in administration, is not perhaps to be expected till some years hence, when the public will look back and see how shamefully they have been deluded, and by what arts they were made to lose the golden opportunity of preventing what they will surely experience — a change of ministers, without a material change of measures, and without any security for a tottering constitution.

But what cares Junius for the security of the constitution? He has now unfolded to us his diabolical principles. As a public man he must ever condemn any measure which may tend accidentally to gratify the sovereign: and Mr. Wilkes is to be supported and assisted in all his attempts (no matter how ridiculous and mischievous his projects) as long as he continues to be a thorn in the king's side! The cause of the country, it seems, in the opinion of Junius, is merely to vex the king; and any rascal is to be supported in any roguery, provided he can only thereby plant a thorn in the king's side. This is the very extremity of faction, and the last degree of political wickedness. Because lord Chatham has been ill-treated by the king, and treacherously betrayed by the duke of Grafton, the latter is to be the pillow on ' which Junius will rest his resentment;' and the public are to oppose the measures of government from mere motives of personal enmity to the sovereign! These are the avowed principles of the man who in the same letter says, ' if ever he should be ' convinced that I had no motive but to destroy ' Wilkes, he shall then be ready to do justice to my ' character, and to declare to the world that he de-' spises me somewhat less than he does at present!' Had I ever acted from personal affection or enmity to Mr. Wilkes, I should justly be despised. But what does he deserve whose avowed motive is personal enmity to the sovereign? The contempt which

I should otherwise feel for the absurdity and glaring inconsistency of Junius, is here swallowed up in my abhorrence of his principle. The right divine and sacredness of kings is to me a senseless jargon. It was thought a daring expression of Oliver Cromwell in the time of Charles the First, that if he found himself placed opposite to the king in battle, he would discharge his piece into his bosom as soon as into any other man's. I go farther: had I lived in those days, I would not have waited for chance to give me an opportunity of doing my duty; I would have sought him through the ranks, and, without the least personal enmity, have discharged my piece into his bosom rather than into any other man's. The king whose actions justify rebellion to his government, deserves death from the hand of every subject. And should such a time arrive, I shall be as free to act as to say. But till then my attachment to the person and family of the sovereign shall ever be found more zealous and sincere than that of his flatterers. I would offend the sovereign with as much reluctance as the parent; but if the happiness and security of the whole family made it necessary, so far, and no farther, I would offend him without remorse.

But let us consider a little whither these principles of Junius would lead us. Should Mr. Wilkes once more commission Mr. Thomas Walpole to procure for him a pension of one thousand pounds upon the Irish establishment for thirty years, he must be supported in the demand by the public, because it would mortify the king!

Should he wish to see lord Rockingham and his friends once more in administration, unclogged by any stipulations for the people, that he might again enjoy a pension of one thousand and forty pounds a year, viz. From the first lord of the treasury, 500l.; from the lords of the treasury, 60l. each; from the lords of trade, 40l. each, &c. the public must give up their attention to points of national benefit, and assist Mr. Wilkes in his attempt, because it would mortify the king!

Should he demand the government of Canada, or of Jamaica, or the embassy to Constantinople; and in case of refusal threaten to write them down, as he had before served another administration, in a year and a half; he must be supported in his pretensions, and upheld in his insolence, because it would mortify the king!

Junius may choose to suppose that these things cannot happen! But that they have happened, notwithstanding Mr. Wilkes's denial, I do aver. I maintain that Mr. Wilkes did commission Mr. Thomas Walpole to solicit for him a pension of one thousand pounds on the Irish establishment for thirty years; with which and a pardon he declared he would be satisfied: and that, notwithstanding his letter to Mr. Onslow, he did accept a clandestine, precarious, and eleemosynary pension from the Rockingham administration; which they paid in proportion to and out of their salaries: and so entirely was it ministerial, that as any of them went out of the ministry, their names were scratched out of the list, and they contributed no longer. I say, he did solicit the governments and the embassy, and threatened their refusal nearly in these words: ' It cost me a year ' and a half to write down the last administration; ' should I employ as much time upon you, very few ' of you would be in at the death.' When these threats did not prevail, he came over to England to embarrass them by his presence; and when he found that lord Rockingham was something firmer and more manly than he expected, and refused to be bullied into what he could not perform, Mr. Wilkes declared that he could not leave England without money; and the duke of Portland and lord Rockingham purchased his absence with one hundred pounds apiece; with which he returned to Paris. And for the truth of what I hear advance, I appeal to the duke of Portland, to lord Rockingham, to lord John Cavendish, to Mr. Walpole, &c. I appeal to the hand-writing of Mr. Wilkes, which is still extant.

Should Mr. Wilkes afterwards (failing in this wholesale trade) choose to dole out his popularity by the pound, and expose the city offices to sale to his brother, his attorney, &c. Junius will tell us, it is only an ambition that he has to make them chamberlain, town-clerk, &c. and he must not be opposed in thus robbing the ancient citizens of their birthright, because any defeat of Mr. Wilkes would gratify the king!

Should he, after consuming the whole of his own fortune and that of his wife, and incurring a debt of twenty thousand pounds merely by his own private extravagance, without a single service or exertion all this time for the public, whilst his estate remained; should he, at length, being undone, commence patriot, have the good fortune to be illegally persecuted, and in consideration of that illegality be espoused by a few gentlemen of the purest public principles; should his debts (though none of them were contracted for the public) and all his other incumbrances be discharged; should he be offered 600l. or 1000l. a year to make him independent for the future; and should he, after all, instead of gratitude for these services, insolently forbid his benefactors to bestow their own money upon any other object but himself, and revile them for setting any bounds to their supplies; Junius (who, any more than lord Chatham, never contributed one farthing to these enormous expences) will tell them, that if they think of converting the supplies of Mr. Wilkes's private extravagance to the support of public measures, they are as great fools as my grandmother, and that Mr. Wilkes ought to hold the strings of their purses as long as he continues to be a thorn in the king's side!

Upon these principles I never have acted, and I never will act. In my opinion, it is less dishonourable to be the creature of a court than the tool of a faction. I will not be either. I understand the two great leaders of opposition to be lord Rockingham and lord Chatham; under one of whose banners all the opposing members of both houses, who desired to get places, enlist. I can place no confidence in either of them, or in any others, unless they will now engage, whilst they are out, to grant certain essential advantages for the security of the public when they shall be in administration. These points they refuse to stipulate, because they are fearful lest they should prevent any future overtures from the court. To force them to these stipulations has been the uniform endeavours of Mr. Sawbridge, Mr. Townsend, Mr. Oliver, &c. and therefore they are abused by Junius. I know no reason but my zeal and industry in the same cause that should entitle me to the honour of being ranked by his abuse with persons of their fortune and station. It is a duty I owe to the memory of the late Mr. Beckford to say, that he had no other aim than this when he provided that sumptuous entertainment at the Mansion-house for the members of both houses in opposition. At that time he drew up the heads of an engagement, which he gave to me with a request that I would couch it in terms so cautious and precise, as to leave no room for future quibble and evasion, but to oblige them either to fulfil the intent of the obligation, or to sign their own infamy, and leave it on record; and this engagement he was determined to propose to them at the Mansion-house, that either by their refusal they might forfeit the confidence of the public, or by the engagement lay a foundation for confidence. When they were informed of the intention, lord Rockingham and his friends flatly refused any engagement; and Mr. Beckford as flatly swore they should then ' eat none of his broth;' and he was determined to put off the entertainment: but Mr. Beckford was prevailed upon by —— to indulge them in the ridiculous parade of a popular procession through the city, and to give them the foolish pleasure of an imaginary consequence, for the real benefit only of the cooks and purveyors.

It was the same motive which dictated the thanks of the city to lord Chatham; which were expressed to be given for his declaration in favour of short parliaments: in order thereby to fix lord Chatham at least to that one constitutional remedy, without which all others can afford no security. The embarrassment, no doubt, was cruel. He had his choice either to offend the Rockingham party, who declared formally against short parliaments, and with the assistance of whose numbers in both houses he must expect again to be minister; or to give up the confidence of the public, from whom finally all real consequence must proceed. Lord Chatham chose the latter: and I will venture to say, that by his answer to those thanks he has given up the people without gaining the friendship or cordial assistance of the Rockingham faction; whose little politics are confined to the making of matches, and extending their family connexions; and who think they gain more by procuring one additional vote to their party in the house of commons, than by adding their languid property and feeble character to the abilities of a Chatham, or the confidence of a public.

Whatever may be the event of the present wretched state of politics in this country, the principles of Junius will suit no form of government. They are not to be tolerated under any constitution. Personal enmity is a motive fit only for the devil. Whoever or whatever is sovereign, demands the respect and support of the people. The union is formed for their happiness, which cannot be had without mutual respect; and he counsels maliciously who would persuade either to a wanton breach of it. When it is banished by either party, and when every method has been tried in vain to restore it, there is no remedy but a divorce: but even then he must have a hard and a wicked heart indeed, who punishes the greatest criminal merely for the sake of the punishment; and who does not let fall a tear for every drop of blood that is shed in a public struggle, however just the quarrel.

JOHN HORNE.

LETTER LIV.

TO

THE PRINTER OF THE PUBLIC ADVERTISER.

SIR, 15 August, 1771.

I OUGHT to make an apology to the duke of Grafton for suffering any part of my attention to be diverted from his grace to Mr. Horne. I am not justified by the similarity of their dispositions. Private vices, however detestable, have not dignity sufficient to attract the censure of the press, unless they are united with the power of doing some signal mischief to the community. Mr. Horne's situation does not correspond with his intentions. In my own opinion (which I know will be attributed to my usual vanity and presumption) his letter to me does not deserve an answer. But I understand that the public are not satisfied with my silence; that an answer is expected from me; and that if I persist in refusing to plead, it will be taken for conviction. I should be inconsistent with the principles I profess, if I declined an appeal to the good sense of the people, or did not willingly submit myself to the judgment of my peers.

If any coarse expressions have escaped me, I am ready to agree that they are unfit for Junius to make use of, but I see no reason to admit that they have been improperly applied.

Mr. Horne, it seems, is unable to comprehend how an extreme want of conduct and discretion can consist with the abilities I have allowed him; nor can he conceive that a very honest man, with a very good understanding, may be deceived by a knave. His knowledge of human nature must be limited indeed. Had he never mixed with the world, one would think that even his books might have taught him better. Did he hear lord Mansfield when he defended his doctrine concerning libels? Or when he stated the law in prosecutions for criminal conversation? Or when he delivered his reasons for calling the house of lords together to receive a copy of his charge to the jury in Woodfall's trial? Had he been present upon any of these occasions, he would have seen how possible it is for a man of the first talents to confound himself in absurdities which would disgrace the lips of an idiot. Perhaps the example might have taught him not to value his own understanding so highly. Lord Littelton's integrity and judgment are unquestionable; yet he is known to admire that cunning Scotchman, and verily believes him an honest man. I speak to facts with which all of us are conversant. I speak to men and to their experience, and will not descend to answer the little sneering sophistries of a collegian. Distinguished talents are not necessarily connected with discretion. If there be any thing remarkable in the character of Mr. Horne, it is, that extreme want of judgment should be united with his very moderate capacity. Yet I have not forgotten the acknowledgment I made him. He owes it to my bounty; and though his letter has lowered him in my opinion, I scorn to retract the charitable donation.

I said it would be very difficult for Mr. Horne to write directly in defence of a ministerial measure, and not be detected; and even that difficulty I confined to his particular situation. He changes the terms of the proposition, and supposes me to assert, that it would be impossible for any man to write for the newspapers and not be discovered.

He repeatedly affirms, or intimates at least, that he knows the author of these letters. With what colour of truth then can he pretend that I am no where to be encountered but in a newspaper? I shall leave him to his suspicions. It is not necessary that I should confide in the honour or discretion of a man who already seems to hate me with as much rancour as if I had formerly been his friend. But he asserts that he has traced me through a variety of signatures. To make the discovery of any importance to his purpose, he should have proved, either that the fictitious character of Junius has not been consistently supported, or that the author has maintained different principles under different signatures. I cannot recall to my memory the numberless trifles I have written; but I rely upon the consciousness of my own integrity, and defy him to fix any colourable charge of inconsistency upon me.

I am not bound to assign the secret motives of his apparent hatred of Mr. Wilkes; nor does it follow that I may not judge fairly of his conduct, though it were true that I had no conduct of my own. Mr. Horne enlarges, with rapture, upon the importance of his services; the dreadful battles which he might have been engaged in, and the dangers he has escaped. In support of the formidable description, he quotes verses without mercy. The gentleman deals in fiction, and naturally appeals to the evidence of the poets. Taking him at his word, he cannot but admit the superiority of Mr. Wilkes in this line of service. On one side we see nothing but imaginary distresses. On the other we see real prosecutions; real penalties; real imprisonment; life repeatedly hazarded; and, at one moment, almost the certainty of death. Thanks are undoubtedly due to every man who does his duty in the engagement; but it is the wounded soldier who deserves the reward.

I did not mean to deny that Mr. Horne had been an active partizan. It would defeat my own purpose not to allow him a degree of merit, which aggravates his guilt. The very charge of contributing his utmost efforts to support a ministerial measure, implies an acknowledgment of his former services. If he had not once been distinguished by his apparent zeal in defence of the common cause, he could not now be distinguished by deserting it. As for myself, it is no longer a question whether I shall mix with the throng, and take a single share in the danger. Whenever Junius appears, he must encounter a host of enemies. But is there no honourable way to serve the public, without engaging in personal quarrels with insignificant individuals, or submitting to the drudgery of canvassing votes for an election? Is there no merit in dedicating my life to the information of my fellow-subjects? What public question have I declined, what villain have I spared? Is there no labour in the composition of these letters? Mr. Horne, I fear, is partial to me, and measures the facility of my writings by the fluency of his own.

He talks to us, in high terms, of the gallant feats he would have performed if he had lived in the last century. The unhappy Charles could hardly have escaped him. But living princes have a claim to his attachment and respect. Upon these terms, there is no danger in being a patriot. If he means any thing more than a pompous rhapsody, let us try how well his argument holds together. I presume he is not yet so much a courtier as to affirm that the constitution has not been grossly and daringly violated under the present reign. He will not say, that the laws have not been shamefully broken or perverted; that the rights of the subject have not been invaded; or that redress has not been repeatedly solicited and refused. Grievances like these were the foundation of the rebellion in the last century, and, if I understand Mr. Horne, they would, at that period, have justified him to his own mind in deliberately attacking the life of his sovereign. I shall not ask him to what political constitution this doctrine can be reconciled. But, at least, it is incumbent upon him to shew, that the present king has better excuses than Charles the First for the errors of his government. He ought to demonstrate to us that the constitution was better understood a hundred years ago than it is at present; that the legal rights of the subject and the limits of the prerogative were more accurately defined, and more clearly comprehended. If propositions like these cannot be fairly maintained, I do not see how he can reconcile it to his conscience, not to act immediately with the same freedom with which he speaks. I reverence the character of Charles the First as little as Mr. Horne; but I will not insult his misfortunes by a comparison that would degrade him.

It is worth observing, by what gentle degrees the furious, persecuting zeal of Mr. Horne has softened into moderation. Men and measures were yesterday his object. What pains did he once take to bring that great state criminal Macquirk to execution! Today he confines himself to measures only. No penal example is to be left to the successors of the duke of Grafton. To-morrow, I presume, both men and measures will be forgiven. The flaming patriot, who so lately scorched us in the meridian, sinks temperately to the west, and is hardly felt as he descends.

I comprehend the policy of endeavouring to communicate to Mr. Oliver and Mr. Sawbridge a share in the reproaches with which he supposes me to have loaded him. My memory fails me, if I have mentioned their names with disrespect; unless it be reproachful to acknowledge a sincere respect for the character of Mr. Sawbridge, and not to have questioned the innocence of Mr. Oliver's intentions.

It seems I am a partizan of the great leader of the opposition. If the charge had been a reproach, it should have been better supported. I did not intend to make a public declaration of the respect I bear lord Chatham. I well knew what unworthy conclusions would be drawn from it. But I am called upon to deliver my opinion, and surely it is not in the little censure of Mr. Horne to deter me from doing signal justice to a man who, I confess, has grown upon my esteem. As for the common

Earl of Chatham

Published by Vernor & Hood, 31 Poultry April 1st 1798

sordid views of avarice, or any purpose of vulgar ambition, I question whether the applause of Junius would be of service to lord Chatham. My vote will hardly recommend him to an increase of his pension, or to a seat in the cabinet. But if his ambition be upon a level with his understanding; if he judges of what is truly honourable for himself, with the same superior genius which animates and directs him to eloquence in debate, to wisdom in decision, even the pen of Junius shall contribute to reward him. Recorded honours shall gather round his monument, and thicken over him. It is a solid fabric, and will support the laurels that adorn it. I am not conversant in the language of panegyric. These praises are extorted from me; but they will wear well, for they have been dearly earned.

My detestation of the duke of Grafton is not founded upon his treachery to any individual: though I am willing enough to suppose that in public affairs it would be impossible to desert or betray lord Chatham, without doing an essential injury to this country. My abhorrence of the duke arises from an intimate knowledge of his character, and from a thorough conviction, that his baseness has been the cause of greater mischief to England than even the unfortunate ambition of lord Bute.

The shortening the duration of parliaments is a subject on which Mr. Horne cannot enlarge too warmly; nor will I question his sincerity. If I did not profess the same sentiments, I should be shamefully inconsistent with myself. It is unnecessary to bind lord Chatham by the written formality of an engagement. He has publicly declared himself a convert to triennial parliaments; and though I have long been convinced that this is the only possible resource we have left to preserve the substantial freedom of the constitution, I do not think we have a right to determine against the integrity of lord Rockingham or his friends. Other measures may undoubtedly be supported in argument, as better adapted to the disorder, or more likely to be obtained.

Mr. Horne is well assured that I never was the champion of Mr. Wilkes. But though I am not obliged to answer for the firmness of his future adherence to the principles he professes, I have no reason to presume that he will hereafter disgrace them. As for all those imaginary cases which Mr.

Horne so petulantly urges against me, I have one plain, honest answer to make to him. Whenever Mr. Wilkes shall be convicted of soliciting a pension, an embassy, or a government, he must depart from that situation, and renounce that character, which he assumes at present, and which, in my opinion, entitle him to the support of the public. By the same act, and at the same moment, he will forfeit his power of mortifying the king; and though he can never be a favourite at St. James's, his baseness may administer a solid satisfaction to the royal mind. The man I speak of has not a heart to feel for the frailties of his fellow-creatures. It is their virtues that afflict, it is their vices that console him.

I give every possible advantage to Mr. Horne when I take the facts he refers to for granted. That they are the produce of his invention, seems highly probable; that they are exaggerated, I have no doubt. At the worst, what do they amount to, but that Mr. Wilkes, who never was thought of as a perfect pattern of morality, has not been at all times proof against the extremity of distress. How shameful is it in a man who has lived in friendship with him, to reproach him with failings, too naturally connected with despair! Is no allowance to be made for banishment and ruin? Does a two years imprisonment make no atonement for his crimes? The resentment of a priest is implacable. No sufferings can soften, no penitence can appease him. Yet he himself, I think, upon his own system, has a multitude of political offences to atone for. I will not insist upon the nauseous detail with which he so long disgusted the public. He seems to be ashamed of it. But what excuse will he make to the friends of the constitution for labouring to promote this consummately bad man to a station of the highest national trust and importance? Upon what honourable motives did he recommend him to the livery of London for their representative; to the ward of Farringdon for their alderman; to the county of Middlesex for their knight? Will he affirm that, at that time, he was ignorant of Mr. Wilkes's solicitations to the ministry? That he should say so, is indeed very necessary for his own justification, but where will he find credulity to believe him?

In what school this gentleman learned his ethics I know not. His logic seems to have been studied under Mr. Dyson. That miserable pamphleteer, by dividing the only precedent in point, and taking as much of it as suited his purpose, had reduced his argument upon the Middlesex election to something like the shape of a syllogism. Mr. Horne has conducted himself with the same ingenuity and candour. I had affirmed that Mr. Wilkes would preserve the public favour ' as long as he stood forth against a ' ministry and parliament, who were doing every ' thing they could to enslave the country, and as ' long as he was a thorn in the king's side.' Yet from the exulting triumph of Mr. Horne's reply, one would think that I had rested my expectation, that Mr. Wilkes would be supported by the public, upon the single condition of his mortifying the king. This may be logic at Cambridge, or at the treasury, but among men of sense and honour it is folly or villany in the extreme.

I see the pitiful advantage he has taken of a single unguarded expression in a letter not intended for the public. Yet it is only the expression that is unguarded. I adhere to the true meaning of that member of the sentence, taken separately as he takes it, and now, upon the coolest deliberation, reassert that, for the purposes I referred to, it may be highly meritorious to the public to wound the personal feelings of the sovereign. It is not a general proposition, nor is it generally applied to the chief magistrate of this, or any other constitution. Mr. Horne knows as well as I do, that the best of princes is not displeased with the abuse which he sees thrown upon his ostensible ministers. It makes them, I presume, more properly the objects of his royal compassion; neither does it escape his sagacity, that the lower they are degraded in the public esteem, the more submissively they must depend upon his favour for protection. This, I affirm upon the most solemn conviction, and the most certain knowledge, is a leading maxim in the policy of the closet. It is unnecessary to pursue the argument any farther.

Mr. Horne is now a very loyal subject. He laments the wretched state of politics in this country, and sees in a new light the weakness and folly of the opposition. Whoever or whatever is sovereign, demands the respect and support of the people[*]; it was not so when Nero fiddled while Rome was burning. Our gracious sovereign has had wonderful success in creating new attachments to his person and family. He owes it, I presume, to the regular system he has pursued in the mystery of conversion. He began with an experiment upon the Scotch, and concludes

[*] The very soliloquy of lord Suffolk before he passed the Rubicon.

with converting Mr. Horne. What a pity it is that the Jews should be condemned by Providence to wait for a Messiah of their own!

The priesthood are accused of misinterpreting the scriptures. Mr. Horne has improved upon his profession. He alters the text, and creates a refutable doctrine of his own. Such artifices cannot long delude the understanding of the people; and, without meaning an indecent comparison, I may venture to foretel, that the Bible and Junius will be read when the commentaries of the Jesuits are forgotten.

J U N I U S.

LETTER LV.

TO
THE PRINTER OF THE PUBLIC ADVERTISER.

SIR, 26 August, 1771.

THE enemies of the people, having now nothing better to object to my friend Junius, are at last obliged to quit his politics, and to rail at him for crimes he is not guilty of. His vanity and impiety are now the perpetual topics of their abuse. I do not mean to lessen the force of such charges (supposing they were true), but to shew that they are not founded. If I admitted the premises, I should readily agree in all the consequences drawn from them. Vanity indeed is a venial error, for it usually carries its own punishment with it; but if I thought Junius capable of uttering a disrespectful word of the religion of his country, I should be the first to renounce and give him up to the public contempt and indignation. As a man, I am satisfied that he is a christian upon the most sincere conviction. As a writer, he would be grossly inconsistent with his political principles, if he dared to attack a religion established by those laws which it seems to be the purpose of his life to defend. Now for the proofs. Junius is accused of an impious allusion to the holy sacrament, where he says that, ' if lord Weymouth ' be denied the cup, there will be no keeping him ' within the pale of the ministry.' Now, sir, I affirm that this passage refers entirely to a ceremonial in the Roman catholic church which denies the cup to the laity. It has no matter of relation to the Protestant creed, and is, in this country, as fair an object of ridicule as transubstantiation, or any other part of lord Peter's history in the Tale of the Tub.

But Junius is charged with equal vanity and impiety in comparing his writings to the holy scripture. The formal protest he makes against any such comparison avails him nothing. It becomes necessary then to shew that the charge destroys itself. If he be vain, he cannot be impious. A vain man does not usually compare himself to an object which it is his design to undervalue. On the other hand, if he be impious, he cannot be vain. For his impiety, if any, must consist in his endeavouring to degrade the holy scriptures by a comparison with his own contemptible writings. This would be folly indeed of the grossest nature, but where lies the vanity? I shall now be told, ' Sir, what you say is ' plausible enough, but still you must allow that it ' is shamefully impudent in Junius to tell us that ' his works will live as long as the Bible.' My answer is, Agreed: but first prove that he has said so. Look at his words, and you will find that the utmost he expects is, that the Bible and Junius will survive the commentaries of the Jesuits, which may prove true in a fortnight. The most malignant sagacity cannot shew that his works are, in his opinion, to live as long as the Bible. Suppose I were to foretel that Jack and Tom would survive Harry. Does it follow that Jack must live as long as Tom? I would only illustrate my meaning, and protest against the least idea of profaneness.

Yet this is the way in which Junius is usually answered, arraigned, and convicted. These candid critics never remember any thing he says in honour of our holy religion; though it is true that one of his leading arguments is made to rest upon the internal evidence which the purest of all religion carries with it. I quote his words, and conclude from them, that he is a true and hearty christian in substance, not in ceremony; though possibly he may not agree with my reverend lords the bishops, or with the head of the church, that prayers are morality, or that kneeling is religion.

PHILO JUNIUS.

LETTER LVI.

FROM

THE REVEREND MR. HORNE TO JUNIUS.

17 August, 1771.

I CONGRATULATE you, sir, on the recovery of your wonted style, though it has cost you a fortnight. I compassionate your labour in the composition of your letters, and will communicate to you the secret of my fluency. Truth needs no ornament; and, in my opinion, what she borrows of the pencil is deformity.

You brought a positive charge against me of corruption. I denied the charge, and called for your proofs. You replied with abuse, and reasserted your charge. I called again for proofs. You reply again with abuse only, and drop your accusation. In your fortnight's letter there is not one word upon the subject of my corruption.

I have no more to say, but to return thanks to you for your condescension, and to a grateful public and honest ministry for all the favours they have conferred upon me. The two latter, I am sure, will never refuse me any grace I shall solicit; and since you have been pleased to acknowledge that you told a deliberate lie in my favour out of bounty, and as a charitable donation, why may I not expect that you will hereafter (if you do not forget you ever mentioned my name with disrepect) make the same acknowledgment for what you have said to my prejudice? This second recantation will perhaps be more abhorrent from your disposition; but should you decline it, you will only afford one more instance how much easier it is to be generous than just, and that men are sometimes bountiful who are not honest.

At all events I am as well satisfied with panegyric as lord Chatham can be. Monument I shall have none; but over my grave it will be said, in your own words, ' Horne's situation did not correspond with ' his intentions ᴾ.'

JOHN HORNE.

ᴾ The epitaph would not be ill suited to the character: at the best, it is but equivocal.

LETTER LVII.

TO

HIS GRACE THE DUKE OF GRAFTON.

MY LORD, 28 September 1771.

The people of England are not apprised of the full extent of their obligations to you. They have yet no adequate idea of the endless variety of your character. They have seen you distinguished and successful in the continued violation of those moral and political duties by which the little as well as the great societies of life are collected and held together. Every colour, every character, became you. With a rate of abilities, which lord Weymouth very justly looks down upon with contempt, you have done as much mischief to the community as Cromwell would have done, if Cromwell had been a coward, and as much as Machiavel, if Machiavel had not known that an appearance of morals and religion are useful in society. To a thinking man, the influence of the crown will, in no view, appear so formidable, as when he observes to what enormous excesses it has safely conducted your grace, without a ray of real understanding, without even the pretensions to common decency or principle of any kind, or a single spark of personal resolution. What must be the operation of that pernicious influence (for which our kings have wisely exchanged the nugatory name of prerogative) that, in the highest stations, can so abundantly supply the absence of virtue, courage, and abilities, and qualify a man to be the minister of a great nation, whom a private gentleman would be ashamed and afraid to admit into his family! Like the universal passport of an ambassador, it supersedes the prohibition of the laws, banishes the staple virtues of the country, and introduces vice and folly triumphantly into all the departments of the state. Other princes, besides his majesty, have had the means of corruption within their reach, but they have used it with moderation. In former times corruption was considered as a foreign auxiliary to government, and only called in upon extraordinary emergencies. The unfeigned piety, the sanctified religion of George the Third, have taught him to new-model the civil forces of the state. The natural resources of the crown are no longer confided in. Corruption glitters in the van; collects and maintains a standing army of mercenaries, and, at the same moment, impoverishes and enslaves the country. His majesty's predecessors (excepting that worthy family from which you, my lord, are unquestionably descended) had some generous qualities in their composition, with vices, I confess, or frailties, in abundance. They were kings or gentlemen, not hypocrites or priests. They were at the head of the church, but did not know the value of their office. They said their prayers without ceremony, and had too little priestcraft in their understanding to reconcile the sanctimonious forms of religion with the utter destruction of the morality of their people. My lord, this is fact, not declamation. With all your partiality to the house of Stuart, you must confess, that even Charles the Second would have blushed at that open encouragement, at those eager, meretricious caresses, with which every species of private vice and public prostitution is received at St. James's. The unfortunate house of Stuart has been treated with an asperity which, if comparison be a defence, seems to border upon injustice. Neither Charles nor his brother were qualified to support such a system of measures as would be necessary to change the government, and subvert the constitution of England. One of them was too much in earnest in his pleasures, the other in his religion. But the danger to this country would cease to be problematical, if the crown should ever descend to a prince whose apparent simplicity might throw his subjects off their guard, who might be no libertine in behaviour, who should have no sense of honour to restrain him, and who, with just religion enough to impose upon the multitude, might have no scruples of conscience to interfere with his morality. With these honourable qualifications, and the decisive advantage of situation, low craft and falsehood are all the abilities that are wanting to destroy the wisdom of ages, and to deface the noblest monument that human policy has erected—I know such a man: my lord, I know you both; and, with the blessing of God (for I too am religious), the people of England shall know you as well as I do. I am not very sure that greater abilities would not in effect be an impediment to a design which seems at first sight to require a superior capacity. A better understanding might make him sensible of the wonderful beauty of that system he was endeavouring to corrupt. The danger of the attempt might alarm him. The meanness, and intrinsic worthlessness of the object (supposing he could attain it), would fill him with shame, repentance, and disgust. But these are sensations which find no entrance into a barbarous, contracted heart. In some men there is a malignant passion to destroy the works of genius, literature, and freedom. The vandal and the monk find equal gratification in it.

Reflections like these, my lord, have a general relation to your grace, and inseparably attend you, in whatever company or situation your character occurs to us. They have no immediate connexion with the following recent fact, which I lay before the public, for the honour of the best of sovereigns, and for the edification of his people.

A prince (whose piety and self-denial, one would think, might secure him from such a multitude of worldly necessities), with an annual revenue of near a million sterling, unfortunately wants money. The navy of England, by an equally strange concurrence of unforeseen circumstances (though not quite so unfortunately for his majesty), is in equal want of timber. The world knows in what a hopeful condition you delivered the navy to your successor, and in what a condition we found it in the moment of distress. You were determined it should continue in the situation in which you left it. It happened, however, very lucky for the privy purse, that one of the above wants promised fair to supply the other. Our religious, benevolent, generous sovereign, has no objection to selling his own timber to his own admiralty, to repair his own ships, nor to putting the money into his own pocket. People of a religious turn naturally adhere to the principles of the church. Whatever they acquire falls into mortmain. Upon a representation from the admiralty of the extraordinary want of timber for the indispensable repairs of the navy, the surveyor-general was directed to make a survey of the timber in all the royal chases and forests in England. Having obeyed his orders with accuracy and attention, he reported, that the finest timber he had any where met with, and the properest in every respect for the purposes of the navy, was in Whittlebury forest, of which your grace, I think, is hereditary ranger. In consequence of this report, the usual warrant was prepared at the treasury, and delivered to the surveyor, by which he or his deputy were authorised to cut down any trees in Whittlebury forest which should appear to be proper for the purposes above mentioned. The deputy being informed that the warrant was signed and delivered to his principal in London, crosses the country to Northamptonshire, and, with an officious zeal for the public service, begins to do his duty in the forest. Unfortunately for him, he had not the warrant in his pocket. The oversight was enormous, and you have punished him for it accordingly. You have insisted that an active useful officer should be dismissed from his place. You have ruined an innocent man and his family. In what language shall I address so black, so cowardly a tyrant; thou worse than one of the Brunswicks, and all the Stuarts! To them who know lord North, it is unnecessary to say, that he was mean and base enough to submit to you. This, however, is but a small part of the fact. After ruining the surveyor's deputy for acting without the warrant, you attack the warrant itself. You declared it was illegal, and swore, in a fit of foaming, frantic passion, that it never should be executed. You asserted, upon your honour, that in the grant of the rangership of Whittlebury forest, made by Charles the second (whom, with a modesty that would do honour to Mr. Rigby, you are pleased to call your ancestor) to one of his bastards (from whom I make no doubt of your descent), the property of the timber is vested in the ranger. I have examined the original grant, and now, in the face of the public, contradict you directly upon the fact. The very reverse of what you have asserted upon your honour is the truth. The grant, expressly and by a particular clause, reserves the property of the timber for the use of the crown. In spite of this evidence, in defiance of the representations of the admiralty, in perfect mockery of the notorious distresses of the English navy, and those equally pressing, and almost equally notorious, necessities of your pious sovereign—here the matter rests. The lords of the treasury recall their warrant; the deputy-surveyor is ruined for doing his duty; Mr. John Pitt (whose name I suppose is offensive to you) submits to be brow-beaten and insulted; the oaks keep their ground; the king is defrauded, and the navy of England may perish for want of the best and finest timber in the island. And all this is submitted to, to appease the duke of Grafton! To gratify the man who has involved the king and his kingdom in confusion and distress, and who, like a treacherous coward, deserted his sovereign in the midst of it!

There has been a strange alteration in your doctrines since you thought it advisable to rob the duke of Portland of his property, in order to strengthen the interest of lord Bute's son-in-law before the last general election. Nullum tempus occurrit regi, was then your boasted motto, and the cry of all your hungry partizans. Now it seems a grant of Charles the Second to one of his bastards is to be held sacred and inviolable! It must not be questioned by the king's servants, nor submitted to any interpretation but your own. My lord, this was not the language you held when it suited you to insult the memory of the glorious deliverer of England from that detested family, to which you are still more nearly allied in principle than in blood. In the name of decency and common sense, what are your grace's merits, either with king or ministry, that should entitle you to assume this domineering authority over both? Is it the fortunate consanguinity you claim with the house of Stuart? Is it the secret correspondence you have for so many years carried on with lord Bute, by the assiduous assistance of your cream-coloured parasite? Could not your gallantry find sufficient employment for him in those gentle offices by which he first acquired the tender friendship of lord Barrington? Or is it only that wonderful sympathy of manners which subsists between your grace and one of your superiors, and does so much honour to you both? Is the union of Blifil and Black George no longer a romance? From whatever origin your influence in this country arises, it is a phenomenon in the history of human virtue and understanding. Good men can hardly believe the fact. Wise men are unable to account for it. Religious men find exercise for their faith, and make it the last effort of their piety, not to repine against Providence.

JUNIUS.

LETTER LVIII.

ADDRESSED TO
THE LIVERY OF LONDON.

GENTLEMEN,   30 September, 1771.

If you alone were concerned in the event of the present election of a chief magistrate of the metropolis, it would be the highest presumption in a stranger to attempt to influence your choice, or even to offer you his opinion. But the situation of public affairs has annexed an extraordinary importance to your resolutions. You cannot, in the choice of your magistrate, determine for yourselves only. You are going to determine upon a point in which every member of the community is interested. I will not scruple to say, that the very being of that law, of that right, of that constitution, for which we have been so long contending, is now at stake. They who would ensnare your judgment, tell you, it is a common, ordinary case, and to be decided by ordinary precedent and practice. They artfully conclude, from moderate peaceable times, to times which are not moderate, and which ought not to be peaceable. While they solicit your favour, they insist upon a rule of rotation which excludes all idea of election.

Let me be honoured with a few minutes of your attention. The question to those who mean fairly to the liberty of the people (which we all profess to have in view) lies within a very narrow compass. Do you mean to desert that just and honourable system of measures which you have hitherto pursued, in hopes of obtaining from parliament or from the crown a full redress of past grievances, and a security for the future? Do you think the cause desperate, and will you declare that you think so to the whole people of England? If this be your meaning and opinion, you will act consistently with it in choosing Mr. Nash. I profess to be unacquainted with his private character. But he has acted as a magistrate, as a public man. As such I speak of him. I see his name in a protest against one of your remonstrances to the crown. He has done every thing in his power to destroy the freedom of popular elections in the city, by publishing the poll upon a former occasion; and I know, in general, that he has distinguished himself by slighting and thwarting all those public measures which you have engaged in with the greatest warmth, and hitherto thought most worthy of your approbation. From his past conduct what conclusion will you draw, but that he will act the same part as lord mayor, which he has invariably acted as alderman and sheriff? I should be sorry to injure the character of a man who perhaps may be honest in his intention, by supposing it possible that he can ever concur with you in any political measure or opinion.

If, on the other hand, you mean to persevere in those resolutions for the public good which, though not always successful, are always honourable, your choice will naturally incline to those men who (whatever they be in other respects) are most likely to cooperate with you in the great purposes which you are determined not to relinquish. The question is not, of what metal your instruments are made, but whether they are adapted to the work you have in hand? The honours of the city, in these times, are improperly, because exclusively, called a reward. You mean not merely to pay, but to employ. Are Mr. Crosby and Mr. Sawbridge likely to execute the extraordinary as well as the ordinary duties of lord mayor? Will they grant you common halls when it shall be necessary? Will they go up with remonstrances to the king? Have they firmness enough to meet the fury of a venal house of commons? Have they fortitude enough not to shrink at imprisonment? Have they spirit enough to hazard their lives and fortunes in a contest, if it should be necessary, with a prostituted legislature? If these questions can fairly be answered in the affirmative, your choice is made. Forgive this passionate language. I am unable to correct it. The subject comes home to us all. It is the language of my heart.

JUNIUS.

LETTER LIX.

TO
THE PRINTER OF THE PUBLIC ADVERTISER.

SIR,   5 October, 1771.

No man laments more sincerely than I do the unhappy differences which have arisen among the friends of the people, and divided them from each other. The cause undoubtedly suffers, as well by the diminution of that strength which union carries with it, as by the separate loss of personal reputation which every man sustains when his character and conduct are frequently held forth in odious or contemptible colours. These differences are only advantageous to the common enemy of the country. The hearty friends of the cause are provoked and disgusted. The lukewarm advocate avails himself of any pretence to relapse into that indolent indifference about every thing that ought to interest an Englishman, so unjustly dignified with the title of moderation. The false, insidious partizan, who creates or foments the disorder, sees the fruit of his dishonest industry ripen beyond his hopes, and rejoices in the promise of a banquet, only delicious to such an appetite as his own. It is time for those who really mean the cause and the people, who have no view to private advantage, and who have virtue enough to prefer the general good of the community to the gratification of personal animosities, it is time for such men to interpose. Let us try whether these fatal dissensions may not yet be reconciled; or, if that be impracticable, let us guard at least against the worst effects of division, and endeavour to persuade these furious partizans, if they will not consent to draw together, to be separately useful to that cause which they all pretend to be attached to. Honour and honesty must not be renounced, although a thousand modes of right and wrong were to occupy the degrees of morality between Zeno and Epicurus. The fundamental principles of christianity may still be preserved though every zealous sectary adheres to his own exclusive doctrine, and pious ecclesiastics make it part of their religion to persecute one another. The civil constitution too, that legal liberty, that general creed, which every Englishman professes, may still be supported, though Wilkes, and Horne, and Townsend, and Sawbridge, should obstinately refuse to communicate, and even if the fathers of the church, if Savile, Richmond, Camden, Rockingham, and Chatham, should disagree in the ceremonies of their political worship, and even in the interpretation of twenty texts in magna charta. I speak to the people as one of the people. Let us employ these men in whatever departments their various abilities are best suited to, and as much to the advantage of the common cause as their different inclinations will permit. They cannot serve us without essentially serving themselves.

If Mr. Nash be elected, he will hardly venture, after so recent a mark of the personal esteem of his fellow-citizens, to declare himself immediately a courtier. The spirit and activity of the sheriffs will, I hope, be sufficient to counteract any sinister intentions of the lord mayor. In collision with their virtue, perhaps he may take fire.

It is not necessary to exact from Mr. Wilkes the virtues of a stoic. They were inconsistent with themselves who, almost at the same moment, represented him as the basest of mankind, yet seemed to expect from him such instances of fortitude and self-denial as would do honour to an apostle. It is not, how-

JOHN WILKES ESQ^r

ever, flattery to say, that he is obstinate, intrepid, and fertile in expedients. That he has no possible resource, but in the public favour, is, in my judgment, a considerable recommendation of him. I wish that every man who pretended to popularity were in the same predicament. I wish that a retreat to St. James's were not so easy and open as patriots have found it. To Mr. Wilkes there is no access. However he may be misled by passion or imprudence, I think he cannot be guilty of a deliberate treachery to the public. The favour of his country constitutes the shield which defends him against a thousand daggers. Desertion would disarm him.

I can more readily admire the liberal spirit and integrity, than the sound judgment of any man, who prefers a republican form of government, in this or any other empire of equal extent, to a monarchy so qualified and limited as ours. I am convinced, that neither is it in theory the wisest system of government, nor practicable in this country. Yet, though I hope the English constitution will for ever preserve its original monarchical form, I would have the manners of the people purely and strictly republican. I do not mean the licentious spirit of anarchy and riot.

I mean a general attachment to the common weal, distinct from any partial attachment to persons or families; an implicit submission to the laws only, and an affection to the magistrate, proportioned to the integrity and wisdom with which he distributes justice to his people, and administers their affairs. The present habit of our political body appears to me the very reverse of what it ought to be. The form of the constitution leans rather more than enough to the popular branch; while, in effect, the manners of the people (of those at least who are likely to take a lead in the country) incline too generally to a dependence upon the crown. The real friends of arbitrary power combine the facts, and are not inconsistent with their principles, when they strenuously support the unwarrantable privileges assumed by the house of commons. In these circumstances, it were much to be desired, that we had many such men as Mr. Sawbridge to represent us in parliament. I speak from common report and opinion only, when I impute to him a speculative predilection in favour of a republic. In the personal conduct and manners of the man I cannot be mistaken. He has shewn himself possessed of that republican firmness which the times require, and by which an English gentleman may be as usefully and as honourably distin-

guished as any citizen of ancient Rome, of Athens, or Lacedæmon.

Mr. Townsend complains, that the public gratitude has not been answerable to his deserts. It is not difficult to trace the artifices which have suggested to him a language so unworthy of his understanding. A great man commands the affections of the people. A prudent man does not complain when he has lost them. Yet they are far from being lost to Mr. Townsend. He has treated our opinion a little too cavalierly. A young man is apt to rely too confidently upon himself, to be as attentive to his mistress as a polite and passionate lover ought to be. Perhaps he found her at first too easy a conquest. Yet, I fancy, she will be ready to receive him whenever he thinks proper to renew his addresses. With all his youth, his spirit, and his appearance, it would be indecent in the lady to solicit his return.

I have too much respect for the abilities of Mr. Horne, to flatter myself that these gentlemen will ever be cordially re-united. It is not, however, unreasonable to expect, that each of them should act his separate part with honour and integrity to the public. As for differences of opinion upon speculative questions, if we wait until they are reconciled, the action of human affairs must be suspended for ever. But neither are we to look for perfection in any one man, nor for agreement among many. When lord Chatham affirms, that the authority of the British legislature is not supreme over the colonies in the same sense in which it is supreme over Great Britain; when lord Camden supposes a necessity (which the king is to judge of), and, founded upon that necessity, attributes to the crown a legal power (not given by the act itself) to suspend the operation of an act of the legislature; I listen to them both with diffidence and respect, but without the smallest degree of conviction or assent. Yet, I doubt not, they delivered their real sentiments, nor ought they to be hastily condemned. I too have a claim to the candid interpretation of my country, when I acknowledge an involuntary compulsive assent to one very unpopular opinion. I lament the unhappy necessity, whenever it arises, of providing for the safety of the state by a temporary invasion of the personal liberty of the subject. Would to God it were practicable to reconcile these important objects in every possible situation of public affairs! I regard the legal liberty of the meanest man in Britain as much as my own, and would defend it with the same zeal. I know we must stand or fall together. But I never can doubt, that the community has a right to command, as well as to purchase, the service of its members. I see that right founded originally upon a necessity which supersedes all argument. I see it established by usage immemorial, and admitted by more than a tacit assent of the legislature. I conclude there is no remedy, in the nature of things, for the grievance complained of; for, if there were, it must long since have been redressed. Though numberless opportunities have presented themselves highly favourable to public liberty, no successful attempt has ever been made for the relief of the subject in this article. Yet it has been felt, and complained of, ever since England had a navy. The conditions which constitute this right must be taken together. Separately, they have little weight. It is not fair to argue from any abuse in the execution, to the illegality of the power; much less is a conclusion to be drawn from the navy to the land service. A seaman can never be employed but against the enemies of his country. The only case in which the king can have a right to arm his subjects in general, is that of a foreign force being actually landed upon our coast. Whenever that case happens, no true Englishman will inquire whether the king's right to compel him to defend his country be the custom of England, or a grant of the legislature. With regard to the press for seamen, it does not follow that the symptoms may not be softened, although the distemper cannot be cured. Let bounties be increased as far as the public purse can support them. Still they have a limit; and when every reasonable expence is incurred, it will be found in fact, that the spur of the press is wanted to give operation to the bounty.

Upon the whole, I never had a doubt about the strict right of pressing, until I heard that lord Mansfield had applauded lord Chatham for delivering something like this doctrine in the house of lords. That consideration staggered me not a little. But, upon reflection, his conduct accounts naturally for itself. He knew the doctrine was unpopular, and was eager to fix it upon the man who is the first object of his fear and detestation. The cunning Scotchman never speaks truth without a fraudulent design. In council he generally affects to take a moderate part. Beside his natural timidity, it makes part of his political plan, never to be known to recommend violent measures. When the guards are called forth to murder their fellow-subjects, it is not by the ostensible advice of lord Mansfield. That odious office, his prudence tells him, is better left to such men as Gower and Weymouth, as Barrington and Grafton. Lord Hillsborough wisely confines his firmness to the distant Americans. The designs of Mansfield are more subtle, more effectual, and secure. Who attacks the liberty of the press? Lord Mansfield. Who invades the constitutional power of juries? Lord Mansfield. What judge ever challenged a juryman, but lord Mansfield? Who was that judge, who, to save the king's brother, affirmed that a man of the first rank and quality, who obtains a verdict in a suit for criminal conversation, is entitled to no greater damages than the meanest mechanic? Lord Mansfield. Who is it makes commissioners of the great seal? Lord Mansfield. Who is it forms a decree for those commissioners, deciding against lord Chatham, and afterwards (finding himself opposed by the judges) declares in parliament, that he never had a doubt that the law was in direct opposition to that decree? Lord Mansfield. Who is he that has made it the study and practice of his life to undermine and alter the whole system of jurisprudence in the court of king's bench? Lord Mansfield. There never existed a man but himself who answered exactly to so complicated a description. Compared to these enormities, his original attachment to the pretender (to whom his dearest brother was confidential secretary) is a virtue of the first magnitude. But the hour of impeachment will come, and neither he nor Grafton shall escape me. Now let them make common cause against England and the house of Hanover. A Stuart and a Murray should sympathise with each other.

When I refer to signal instances of unpopular opinions delivered and maintained by men who may well be supposed to have no view but the public good, I do not mean to renew the discussion of such opinions. I should be sorry to revive the dormant questions of stamp-act, corn-bill, or press-warrant. I mean only to illustrate one useful proposition, which it is the intention of this paper to inculcate; ' That ' we should not generally reject the friendship or ser- ' vices of any man, because he differs from us in a ' particular opinion.' This will not appear a superfluous caution, if we observe the ordinary conduct of mankind. In public affairs there is the least chance of a perfect concurrence of sentiment or inclination. Yet every man is able to contribute something to the common stock, and no man's contribution should be rejected. If individuals have no virtues, their vices may be of use to us. I care not with what principle the new-born patriot is animated, if the measures he supports are beneficial to the community. The nation is interested in his conduct. His motives are his own. The properties of a patriot are perishable in the individual, but there is a quick succession of subjects, and the breed is worth preserving. The spirit of the Americans may be an useful example to us. Our dogs and horses are only English upon English ground; but patriotism, it seems, may be improved by transplanting. I will not reject a bill which tends to confine parliamentary privilege within reasonable bounds, though it should be stolen from the house of Cavendish, and introduced by Mr. Onslow. The features of the infant are a proof of the descent, and vindicate the noble birth from the baseness of the adoption. I willingly accept of a sarcasm from colonel Barré, or a simile from Mr. Burke. Even the silent vote of Mr. Calcraft is worth reckoning in a division. What though he riots in the plunder of the army, and has only determined to be a patriot, when he could not be a peer? Let us profit by the assistance of such men while they are with us, and place them, if it be possible, in the post of danger, to prevent desertion. The wary Wedderburne, the pompous Suffolk, never threw away the scabbard, nor ever went upon a forlorn hope. They always treated the king's servants as men with whom, some time or other, they might possibly be in friendship. When a man who stands forth for the public, has gone that length from which there is no practicable retreat; when he has given that kind of personal offence which a pious monarch never pardons, I then begin to think him in earnest, and that he never will have occasion to solicit the forgiveness of his country. But instances of a determination so entire and unreserved are rarely met with. Let us take mankind as they are. Let us distribute the virtues and abilities of individuals according to the offices they affect, and when they quit the service, let us endeavour to supply their places with better men than we have lost. In this country there are always candidates enough for popular favour. The temple of fame is the shortest passage to riches and preferment.

Above all things, let me guard my countrymen against the meanness and folly of accepting of a trifling or moderate compensation for extraordinary and essential injuries. Our enemies treat us as the cunning trader does the unskilful Indian. They magnify their generosity when they give us baubles of little proportionate value for ivory and gold. The same house of commons who robbed the constituent body of their right of free election; who presumed to make a law under pretence of declaring it; who paid our good king's debts, without once inquiring how they were incurred; who gave thanks for re-repeated murders committed at home, and for national infamy incurred abroad; who screened lord Mansfield; who imprisoned the magistrates of the metropolis for asserting the subject's right to the protection of the laws; who erased a judicial record, and ordered all proceedings in a criminal suit to be suspended; this very house of commons have graciously consented, that their own members may be compelled to pay their debts, and that contested elections shall for the future be determined with some decent regard to the merits of the case. The event of the suit is of no consequence to the crown. While parliaments are septennial, the purchase of the sitting member or of the petitioner makes but the difference of a day. Concessions such as these are of little moment to the sum of things, unless it be to prove that the worst of men are sensible of the injuries they have done us, and perhaps to demonstrate to us the imminent danger of our situation. In the shipwreck of the state trifles float and are preserved; while every thing solid and valuable sinks to the bottom, and is lost for ever.

JUNIUS.

LETTER LX.

TO

THE PRINTER OF THE PUBLIC ADVERTISER.

SIR,   15 October, 1771.

I AM convinced that Junius is incapable of wilfully misrepresenting any man's opinion, and that his inclination leads him to treat lord Camden with particular candour and respect. The doctrine attributed to him by Junius, as far as it goes, corresponds with that stated by your correspondent Scævola, who seems to make a distinction without a difference. Lord Camden, it is agreed, did certainly maintain that, in the recess of parliament, the king (by which we all mean the king in council, or the executive power) might suspend the operation of an act of the legislature; and he founded his doctrine upon a supposed necessity, of which the king, in the first instance, must be judge. The lords and commons cannot be judges of it in the first instance, for they do not exist. Thus far Junius.

But, says Scævola, lord Camden made parliament, and not the king, judges of the necessity. That parliament may review the acts of ministers is unquestionable: but there is a wide difference between saying that the crown has a legal power, and that ministers may act at their peril. When we say an act is illegal, we mean that it is forbidden by a joint resolution of the three estates. How a subsequent resolution of two of those branches can make it legal ab initio, will require explanation. If it could, the consequence would be truly dreadful, especially in these times. There is no act of arbitrary power which the king might not attribute to necessity, and for which he would not be secure of obtaining the approbation of his prostituted lords and commons. If lord Camden admits that the subsequent sanction of parliament was necessary to make the proclamation legal, why did he so obstinately oppose the bill which was soon after brought in for indemnifying all those persons who had acted under it? If that bill had not been passed, I am ready to maintain, in direct contradiction to lord Camden's doctrine (taken as Scævola states it), that a litigious exporter of corn, who had suffered in his property in consequence of the proclamation, might have laid his action against the custom-house officers, and would infallibly have recovered damages. No jury could refuse them; and if I, who am by no means litigious, had been so injured, I would assuredly have instituted a suit in Westminster-hall, on purpose to try the question of right. I would have done it upon a principle of defiance of the pretended power of either or both houses to make declarations inconsistent with law, and I have no doubt that, with an act of parliament on my side, I should have been too strong for them all. This is the way in which an Englishman should speak and act, and not suffer dangerous precedents to be established because the circumstances are favourable or palliating.

With regard to lord Camden, the truth is, that he inadvertently over-shot himself, as appears plainly by that unguarded mention of a tyranny of forty days, which I myself heard. Instead of asserting that the proclamation was legal, he should have said, ' My ' lords, I know the proclamation was illegal, but ' I advised it because it was indispensably neces- ' sary to save the kingdom from famine, and I sub- ' mit myself to the justice and mercy of my coun- ' try.'

Such language as this would have been manly,

rational, and consistent: not unfit for a lawyer, and every way worthy of a great man.

PHILO JUNIUS.

P. S. If Scævola should think proper to write again upon this subject, I beg of him to give me a direct answer, that is, a plain affirmative or negative, to the following questions:—In the interval between the publishing such a proclamation (or order of council) as that in question, and its receiving the sanction of the two houses, of what nature is it—is it legal or illegal; or is it neither one nor the other? I mean to be candid, and will point out to him the consequence of his answer either way. If it be legal, it wants no farther sanction. If it be illegal, the subject is not bound to obey it, consequently it is a useless, nugatory act, even as to its declared purpose. Before the meeting of parliament the whole mischief which it means to prevent will have been completed.

LETTER LXI.

TO

Z E N O.

SIR, 17 October, 1771.

THE sophistry of your letter in defence of lord Mansfield is adapted to the character you defend. But lord Mansfield is a man of form, and seldom in his behaviour transgresses the rules of decorum. I shall imitate his lordship's good manners, and leave you in the full possession of his principles. I will not call you liar, jesuit, or villain, but, with all the politeness imaginable, perhaps I may prove you so.

Like other fair pleaders in lord Mansfield's school of justice, you answer Junius by misquoting his words, and mistating his propositions. If I am candid enough to admit that this is the very logic taught at St. Omer's, you will readily allow that it is the constant practice in the court of king's bench. Junius does not say, that he never had a doubt about the strict right of pressing, till he knew lord Mansfield was of the same opinion. His words are, ' until ' he heard that lord Mansfield had applauded lord ' Chatham for maintaining that doctrine in the ' house of lords.' It was not the accidental concurrence of lord Mansfield's opinion, but the suspicious applause given by a cunning Scotchman to the man he detests, that raised and justified a doubt in the mind of Junius. The question is not, whether lord Mansfield be a man of learning and abilities (which Junius has never disputed), but whether or no he abuses and misapplies his talents.

Junius did not say that lord Mansfield had advised the calling out the guards. On the contrary, his plain meaning is, that he left that odious office to men less cunning than himself. Whether lord Mansfield's doctrine concerning libels be or be not an attack upon the liberty of the press, is a question which the public in general are very well able to determine. I shall not enter into it at present. Nor do I think it necessary to say much to a man who had the daring confidence to say to a jury, ' Gentlemen, ' you are to bring in a verdict guilty or not guilty; ' but whether the defendant be guilty or innocent is

' not matter for your consideration.' Clothe it in what language you will, this is the sum total of lord Mansfield's doctrine. If not, let Zeno shew us the difference.

But it seems the liberty of the press may be abused, and the abuse of a valuable privilege is the certain means to lose it. The first I admit, but let the abuse be submitted to a jury—a sufficient, and indeed the only legal and constitutional, check upon the license of the press. The second I flatly deny. In direct contradiction to lord Mansfield, I affirm that ' the abuse of a valuable privilege is not the ' certain means to lose it.' If it were, the English nation would have few privileges left; for where is the privilege that has not, at one time or other, been abused by individuals? But it is false in reason and equity, that particular abuses should produce a general forfeiture. Shall the community be deprived of the protection of the laws because there are robbers and murderers? Shall the community be punished because individuals have offended? Lord Mansfield says so, consistently enough with his principles, but I wonder to find him so explicit. Yet, for one concession, however extorted, I confess myself obliged to him. The liberty of the press is, after all, a valuable privilege. I agree with him most heartily, and will defend it against him.

You ask me, What juryman was challenged by lord Mansfield? I tell you his name was Benson. When his name was called, lord Mansfield ordered the clerk to pass him by. As for his reasons, you may ask himself, for he assigned none. But I can tell you what all men thought of it. This Benson had been refractory upon a former jury, and would not accept of the law as delivered by lord Mansfield; but had the impudence to pretend to think for himself. But you, it seems, honest Zeno, know nothing of the matter! You never read Junius's letter to your patron! You never heard of the intended instructions from the city to impeach lord Mansfield! You never heard by what dexterity of Mr. Paterson that measure was prevented! How wonderfully ill some people are informed!

Junius did never affirm that the crime of seducing the wife of a mechanic or a peer is not the same, taken in a moral or religious view. What he affirmed in contradiction to the levelling principle so lately adopted by lord Mansfield was, ' that the da-
' mages should be proportioned to the rank and for-

' tune of the parties :' and for this plain reason (admitted by every other judge that ever sat in Westminster-hall) because, what is a compensation or penalty to one man is none to another. The sophistical distinction you attempt to draw between the person injured and the person injuring is Mansfield all over. If you can once establish the proposition, that the injured party is not entitled to receive large damages, it follows pretty plainly that the party injuring should not be compelled to pay them; consequently the king's brother is effectually screened by lord Mansfield's doctrine. Your reference to Nathan and David comes naturally in aid of your patron's professed system of jurisprudence. He is fond of introducing into the court of king's bench any law that contradicts or excludes the common law of England; whether it be canon, civil, jus gentium, or levitical. But, sir, the bible is the code of our religious faith, not of our municipal jurisprudence: and though it was the pleasure of God to inflict a particular punishment upon David's crime (taken as a breach of his divine commands), and to send his prophet to denounce it, an English jury have nothing to do either with David or the prophet. They consider the crime only as it is a breach of order, an injury to an individual, and an offence to society, and they judge of it by certain positive rules of law, or by the practice of their ancestors. Upon the whole, the man after God's own heart is much indebted to you for comparing him to the duke of Cumberland. That his royal highness may be the man after lord Mansfield's own heart, seems much more probable, and you, I think, Mr. Zeno, might succeed tolerably well in the character of Nathan. The evil deity, the prophet, and the royal sinner, would be very proper company for one another.

You say lord Mansfield did not make the commissioners of the great seal, and that he only advised the king to appoint. I believe Junius meant no more, and the distinction is hardly worth disputing.

You say he did not deliver an opinion upon lord Chatham's appeal. I affirm that he did, directly in favour of the appeal. This is a point of fact, to be determined by evidence only. But you assign no reason for his supposed silence, nor for his desiring a conference with the judges the day before. Was not all Westminster Hall convinced that he did it with a view to puzzle them with some perplexing question, and in hopes of bringing some of them over to him? You say the commissioners were very capable of framing a decree for themselves. By the fact it only appears, that they were capable of framing an illegal one, which, I apprehend, is not much to the credit either of their learning or integrity.

We are both agreed that lord Mansfield has incessantly laboured to introduce new modes of proceeding in the court where he presides; but you attribute it to an honest zeal in behalf of innocence oppressed by quibble and chicane. I say that he has introduced new law too, and removed the land-marks established by former decisions. I say that his view is to change a court of common law into a court of equity, and to bring every thing within the arbitrium of a prætorian court. The public must determine between us. But now for his merits. First, then, the establishment of the judges in their places for life (which you tell us was advised by lord Mansfield), was a concession merely to catch the people. It bore the appearance of a royal bounty, but had nothing real in it. The judges were already for life, excepting in the case of a demise. Your boasted bill only provides that it shall not be in the power of the king's successor to remove them. At the best, therefore, it is only a legacy, not a gift, on the part of his present majesty, since for himself he gives up nothing. That he did oppose lord Camden and lord Northington upon the proclamation against the exportation of corn, is most true, and with great ability. With his talents, and taking the right side of so clear a question, it was impossible to speak ill. His motives are not so easily penetrated. They who are acquainted with the state of politics at that period, will judge of them somewhat differently from Zeno. Of the popular bills, which you say he supported in the house of lords, the most material is unquestionably that of Mr. Grenville for deciding contested elections. But I should be glad to know upon what possible pretence any member of the upper house could oppose such a bill after it had passed the house of commons? I do not pretend to know what share he had in promoting the other two bills, but I am ready to give him all the credit you desire. Still you will find that a whole life of deliberate iniquity is ill atoned for by doing now and then a laudable action upon a mixed or doubtful principle. If it be unworthy of him, thus ungratefully treated, to labour any longer for the public, in God's name let him retire. His brother's patron (whose health he once was anxious for) is dead, but the son of that unfortunate prince survives, and, I dare say, will be ready to receive him.

PHILO JUNIUS.

LETTER LXII.

TO
AN ADVOCATE IN THE CAUSE OF THE PEOPLE.

SIR, 18 October, 1771.

You do not treat Junius fairly. You would not have condemned him so hastily if you had ever read judge Foster's argument upon the legality of pressing seamen. A man who has not read that argument is not qualified to speak accurately upon the subject. In answer to strong facts and fair reasoning, you produce nothing but a vague comparison between two things which have little or no resemblance to each other. General warrants, it is true, had been often issued, but they had never been regularly questioned or resisted until the case of Mr. Wilkes. He brought them to trial, and the moment they were tried they were declared illegal. This is not the case of press warrants. They have been complained of, questioned, and resisted, in a thousand instances; but still the legislature have never interposed, nor has there ever been a formal decision against them in any of the superior courts. On the contrary, they have been frequently recognized and admitted by parliament, and there are judicial opinions given in their favour by judges of the first character. Under the various circumstances stated by Junius, he has a right to conclude, for himself, that there is no remedy. If you have a good one to propose you may depend upon the assistance and applause of Junius. The magistrate who guards the liberty of the individual, deserves to be commended. But let him remember that it is also his duty to provide for, or at least not to hazard, the safety of the community. If in the case of a foreign war and the expectation of an invasion, you would rather keep your fleet in harbour than man it by pressing seamen who refuse the bounty, I have done.

You talk of disbanding the army with wonderful ease and indifference. If a wiser man held such language, I should be apt to suspect his sincerity.

As for keeping up a much greater number of seamen in time of peace, it is not to be done. You will oppress the merchant, you will distress trade, and destroy the nursery of your seamen. He must be a miserable statesman who voluntarily by the same act increases the public expence, and lessens the means of supporting it.

PHILO JUNIUS.

LETTER LXIII.

22 October, 1771.

A FRIEND of Junius desires it may be observed (in answer to A Barrister at Law),

1. That the fact of lord Mansfield's having ordered a juryman to be passed by (which poor Zeno never heard of) is now formally admitted. When Mr. Benson's name was called, lord Mansfield was observed to flush in the face (a signal of guilt not uncommon with him), and cried out, Pass him by. This I take to be something more than a peremptory challenge. It is an unlawful command, without any reason assigned. That the council did not resist is true; but this might happen either from inadvertence, or a criminal complaisance to lord Mansfield. You barristers are too apt to be civil to my lord chief justice, at the expence of your clients.

2. Junius did never say that lord Mansfield had destroyed the liberty of the press. ' That his lord-

' ship has laboured to destroy; that his doctrine is
' an attack upon the liberty of the press; that it is
' an invasion of the right of juries,' are the propositions maintained by Junius. His opponents never answer him in point, for they never meet him fairly upon his own ground.

3. Lord Mansfield's policy, in endeavouring to screen his unconstitutional doctrines behind an act of the legislature, is easily understood. Let every Englishman stand upon his guard; the right of juries to return a general verdict, in all cases whatsoever, is a part of our constitution. It stands in no need of a bill either enacting or declaratory to confirm it.

4. With regard to the Grosvenor cause, it is pleasant to observe that the doctrine attributed by Junius to lord Mansfield is admitted by Zeno, and directly defended. The Barrister has not the assurance to deny it flatly, but he evades the charge, and softens the doctrine by such poor, contemptible quibbles, as cannot impose upon the meanest understanding.

5. The quantity of business in the court of King's

Bench proves nothing but the litigious spirit of the people, arising from the great increase of wealth and commerce. These, however, are now upon the decline, and will soon leave nothing but law-suits behind them. When Junius affirms that lord Mansfield has laboured to alter the system of jurisprudence in the court where his lordship presides, he speaks to those who are able to look a little farther than the vulgar. Besides that the multitude are easily deceived by the imposing names of equity and substantial justice, it does not follow that a judge who introduces into his court new modes of procceding, and new principles of law, intends, in every instance, to decide unjustly. Why should he where he has no interest? We say that lord Mansfield is a bad man, and a worse judge; but we do not say that he is a mere devil. Our adversaries would fain reduce us to the difficulty of proving too much. This artifice, however, shall not avail him. The truth of the matter is plainly this. When lord Manfield has succeeded in his scheme of changing a court of common law to a court of equity, he will have it in his power to do injustice whenever he thinks proper. This, though a wicked purpose, is neither absurd not unattainable.

6. The last paragraph, relative to lord Chatham's cause, cannot be answered. It partly refers to facts, of too secret a nature to be ascertained, and partly is unintelligible. ' Upon one point the cause is de-
' cided against lord Chatham. Upon another point
' it is decided for him.' Both the law and the language are well suited to a barrister! If I have any guess at this honest gentleman's meaning, it is, that, ' whereas the commissioners of the great seal
' saw the question in a point of view unfavourable
' to lord Chatham, and decreed accordingly; lord
' Mansfield, out of sheer love and kindness to lord
' Chatham, took the pains to place it in a point of
' view more favourable to the appellant.' Credat Judæus Apella. So curious an assertion would stagger the faith of Mr. Sylva.

LETTER LXIV.

2 November, 1771.

We are desired to make the following declaration, in behalf of Junius, upon three material points, on which his opinion has been mistaken, or misrepresented.

1. Junius considers the right of taxing the colonies, by an act of the British legislature, as a speculative right merely, never to be exerted, nor ever to be renounced. To his judgment it appears plain, ' That the general reasonings, which were employed ' against that power, went directly to our whole le-
' gislative right, and that one part of it could not be
' yielded to such arguments, without a virtual sur-
' render of all the rest.'

2. That, with regard to press-warrants, his argument should be taken in his own words, and answered strictly; that comparisons may sometimes illustrate, but prove nothing; and that, in this case,

an appeal to the passions is unfair and unnecessary. Junius feels and acknowledges the evil in the most express terms, and will shew himself ready to concur in any rational plan that may provide for the liberty of the individual, without hazarding the safety of the community. At the same time he expects that the evil, such as it is, be not exaggerated or misrepresented. In general, it is not unjust that, when the rich man contributes his wealth, the poor man should serve the state in person; otherwise the latter contributes nothing to the defence of that·law and constitution from which he demands safety and protection. But the question does not lie between rich and poor. The laws of England make no such distinctions. Neither is it true that the poor man is torn from the care and support of a wife and family, helpless without him. The single question is, whether the man [q], in times of public danger, shall serve the merchant or the state, in that profession to which he was bred, and by the exercise of which alone he can honestly support himself and his family. General arguments against the doctrine of necessity, and the dangerous use that may be made of it, are of no weight in this particular case. Necessity in-

[q] I confine myself strictly to seamen; if any others are pressed, it is a gross abuse, which the magistrate can and should correct.

cludes the idea of inevitable. Whenever it is so, it creates a law, to which all positive laws and all positive rights must give way. In this sense the levy of ship-money by the king's warrant was not necessary, because the business might have been as well or better done by parliament. If the doctrine, maintained by Junius, be confined within this limitation, it will go but very little way in support of arbitrary power. That the king is to judge of the occasion, is no objection, unless we are told how it can possibly be otherwise. There are other instances not less important in the exercise, nor less dangerous in the abuse, in which the constitution relies entirely upon the king's judgment. The executive power proclaims war and peace, binds the nation by treaties, orders general embargoes, and imposes quarantines, not to mention a multitude of prerogative writs, which, though liable to the greatest abuses, were never disputed.

3. It has been urged, as a reproach to Junius, that he has not delivered an opinion upon the game laws, and particularly the late dog act. But Junius thinks he has much greater reason to complain, that he is never assisted by those who are able to assist him, and that almost the whole labour of the press

is thrown upon a single hand, from which a discussion of every public question whatsoever is unreasonably expected. He is not paid for his labour, and certainly has a right to choose his employment. As to the game laws, he never scrupled to declare his opinion, that they are a species of the forest laws, that they are oppressive to the subject, and that the spirit of them is incompatible with legal liberty: that the penalties imposed by these laws bear no proportion to the nature of the offence, that the mode of trial and the degree and kind of evidence necessary to convict, not only deprive the subject of all the benefits of a trial by jury, but are in themselves too summary, and to the last degree arbitrary and oppressive. That, in particular, the late acts to prevent dog-stealing, or killing game between sun and sun, are distinguished by their absurdity, extravagance, and pernicious tendency. If these terms are weak, or ambiguous, in what language can Junius express himself? It is no excuse for lord Mansfield to say that he happened to be absent when these bills passed the house of lords. It was his duty to be present. Such bills could never have passed the house of commons without his knowledge. But we very well know by what rule he regulates his attendance. When that order was made in the house of lords in the case of lord Pomfret, at which every Englishman shudders, my honest lord Mansfield found himself, by mere accident, in the court of king's bench. Otherwise he would have done wonders in defence of law and property! The pitiful evasion is adapted to the character. But Junius will never justify himself by the example of this bad man. The distinction between doing wrong, and avoiding to do right, belongs to lord Mansfield. Junius disclaims it.

LETTER LXV.

TO

LORD CHIEF JUSTICE MANSFIELD.

2 November, 1771.

AT the intercession of three of your countrymen you have bailed a man who, I presume, is also a Scotchman, and whom the lord mayor of London had refused to bail. I do not mean to enter into an examination of the partial, sinister motives of your conduct; but confining myself strictly to the fact, I affirm that you have done that which by law you were not warranted to do. The thief was taken in the theft, the stolen goods were found upon him, and he made no defence. In these circumstances (the truth of which you dare not deny, because it is of public notoriety) it could not stand indifferent whether he was guilty or not, much less could there be any presumption of his innocence; and in these circumstances I affirm, in contradiction to YOU, lord chief justice Mansfield, that by the laws of England he was not bailable. If ever Mr. Eyre should be brought to trial, we shall hear what you have to say for yourself; and I pledge myself, before God and my country, in proper time and place to make good my charge against you.

JUNIUS.

LETTER LXVI.

TO

THE PRINTER OF THE PUBLIC ADVERTISER.

9 November, 1771.

JUNIUS engages to make good his charge against lord chief justice Mansfield some time before the meeting of parliament, in order that the house of commons may, if they think proper, make it one article in the impeachment of the said lord chief justice.

LETTER LXVII.

TO

HIS GRACE THE DUKE OF GRAFTON.

27 November, 1771.

WHAT is the reason, my lord, that, when almost every man in the kingdom, without distinction of principles or party, exults in the ridiculous defeat of sir James Lowther, when good and bad men unite in one common opinion of that baronet, and triumph in his distress, as if the event (without any reference to vice or virtue) were interesting to human nature, your grace alone should appear so miserably depressed and afflicted? In such universal joy, I know not where you will look for a compliment of condolence, unless you appeal to the tender, sympathetic sorrows of Mr. Bradshaw. That cream-coloured gentleman's tears, affecting as they are, carry consolation along with them. He never weeps but like an April shower, with a lambent ray of sunshine upon his countenance. From the feelings of honest men, upon this joyful occasion, I do not mean to draw any conclusion to your grace. They naturally rejoice when they see a signal instance of tyranny resisted with success; of treachery exposed to the derision of the world; an infamous informer defeated, and an impudent robber dragged to the public gibbet. But in the other class of mankind, I own, I expected to meet the duke of Grafton. Men who have no regard for justice, nor any sense of honour, seem as heartily pleased with sir James Lowther's well deserved punishment, as if it did not constitute an example against themselves. The unhappy baronet has no friends, even among those who resemble him. You, my lord, are not reduced to so deplorable a state of dereliction. Every villain in the kingdom is your friend; and, in compliment to such amity, I think you should suffer your dismal countenance to clear up. Besides, my lord, I am a little anxious for the consistency of your character. You violate your own rules of decorum when you do not insult the man whom you have betrayed.

The divine justice of retribution seems now to have begun its progress. Deliberate treachery entails punishment upon the traitor. There is no possibility of escaping it, even in the highest rank to which the consent of society can exalt the meanest and worst of men. The forced, unnatural union of Luttrell and Middlesex was an omen of another unnatural union, by which indefeasible infamy is attached to the house of Brunswick. If one of those acts was virtuous and honourable, the best of princes, I thank God, is happily rewarded for it by the other. Your grace, it has been said, had some share in recommending Colonel Luttrell to the king; or was it only the gentle Bradshaw who made himself answerable for the good behaviour of his friend? An intimate connexion has long subsisted between him and the worthy lord Irnham. It arose from a fortunate similarity of principles, cemented by the constant mediation of their common friend Miss Davis[r].

---

[r] There is a certain family in this country on which nature seems to have entailed an hereditary baseness of disposition. As far as their history has been known, the son has regularly improved upon the vices of his father, and has taken care to transmit them

Yet I confess I should be sorry that the opprobrious infamy of this match should reach beyond the family. We have now a better reason than ever to pray for the long life of the best of princes, and the

pure and undeminished into the bosom of his successor. In the senate their abilities have confined them to those humble, sordid services, in which the scavengers of the ministry are usually employed. But in the memoirs of private treachery they stand first and unrivalled. The following story will serve to illustrate the character of this respectable family, and to convince the world that the present possessor has as clear a title to the infamy of his ancestors, as he has to their estate. It deserves to be recorded for the curiosity of the fact, and should be given to the public as a warning to every honest member of society.

The present lord, who is now in the decline of life, lately cultivated the acquaintance of a younger brother of a family with which he had lived in some degree of intimacy and friendship. The young man had long been the dupe of a most unhappy attachment to a common prostitute. His friends and relations foresaw the consequence of this connexion, and did every thing that depended upon them to save him from ruin. But he had a friend in his lordship, whose advice rendered all their endeavours ineffectual. This hoary letcher, not contented with the enjoyment of his friend's mistress, was base enough to take advantage of the passions and folly of a young man, and persuaded him to marry her. He descended even to perform the office of father to the prostitute. He gave her to his friend, who was on the point of leaving the kingdom, and the next night lay with her himself.

Whether the depravity of the human heart can produce any thing more base and detestable than this fact, must be left undetermined until the son shall arrive at his father's age and experience.

welfare of his royal issue. I will not mix any thing ominous with my prayers; but let parliament look to it. A Luttrell shall never succeed to the crown of England. If the hereditary virtues of the family deserve a kingdom, Scotland will be a proper retreat for them.

The next is a most remarkable instance of the goodness of Providence. The just law of retaliation has at last overtaken the little, contemptible tyrant of the north. To this son-in-law of your dearest friend the earl of Bute, you meant to transfer the duke of Portland's property; and you hastened the grant, with an expedition unknown, to the treasury, that he might have it time enough to give a decisive turn to the election for the county. The immediate consequence of this flagitious robbery was, that he lost the election, which you meant to insure to him, and with such signal circumstances of scorn, reproach, and insult (to say nothing of the general exultation of all parties), as (excepting the king's brother-in-law, colonel Luttrell, and old Simon his father-in-law) hardly ever fell upon a gentleman in this country. In the event he loses the very property of which he thought he had gotten possession, and after an expence which would have paid the value of the land in question twenty times over. The forms of villany, you see, are necessary to its success. Hereafter you will act with greater circumspection, and not drive so directly to your object. To snatch a grace, beyond the reach of common treachery, is an exception, not a rule.

And now, my good lord, does not your conscious heart inform you, that the justice of retribution begins to operate, and that it may soon approach your person? Do you think that Junius has renounced the Middlesex election? Or that the king's timber shall be refused to the royal navy with impunity? Or that you shall hear no more of the sale of that patent to Mr. Hine which you endeavoured to screen by suddenly dropping your prosecution of Samuel Vaughan, when the rule against him was made absolute? I believe, indeed, there never was such an instance in all the history of negative impudence. But it shall not save you. The very sunshine you live in is a prelude to your dissolution. When you are ripe you shall be plucked.

JUNIUS.

P. S. I beg you will convey to our gracious master my humble congratulations upon the glorious success of peerages and pensions, so lavishly distributed as the rewards of Irish virtue.

LETTER LXVIII.

TO

LORD CHIEF JUSTICE MANSFIELD.

21 January, 1772.

I HAVE undertaken to prove that when, at the intercession of three of your countrymen, you bailed John Eyre, you did that which by law you were not warranted to do, and that a felon, under the circumstances of being taken in the fact, with the stolen goods upon him, and making no defence, is not bailable by the laws of England. Your learned advocates have interpreted this charge into a denial

Earl Mansfield

that the court of king's bench, or the judges of that court during the vacation, have any greater authority to bail for criminal offences than a justice of peace. With the instance before me, I am supposed to question your power of doing wrong, and to deny the existence of a power at the same moment that I arraign the illegal exercise of it. But the opinions of such men, whether wilful in their malignity, or sincere in their ignorance, are unworthy of my notice. You, lord Mansfield, did not understand me so, and, I promise you, your cause requires an abler defence. I am now to make good my charge against you. However dull my argument, the subject of it is interesting. I shall be honoured with the attention of the public, and have a right to demand the attention of the legislature. Supported, as I am, by the whole body of the criminal law of England, I have no doubt of establishing my charge. If, on your part, you should have no plain, substantial defence, but should endeavour to shelter yourself under the quirk and evasion of a practising lawyer, or under the mere insulting assertion of power without right, the reputation you pretend to is gone for ever; you stand degraded from the respect and authority of your office, and are no longer de jure, lord chief justice of England. This letter, my lord, is addressed, not so much to you, as to the public. Learned as you are, and quick in apprehension, few arguments are necessary to satisfy you, that you have done that which by law you were not warranted to do. Your conscience already tells you, that you have sinned against knowledge, and that whatever defence you make contradicts your own internal conviction. But other men are willing enough to take the law upon trust. They rely upon your authority, because they are too indolent to search for information; or, conceiving that there is some mystery in the laws of their country, which lawyers are only qualified to explain, they distrust their judgment, and voluntarily renounce the right of thinking for themselves. With all the evidence of history before them, from Tresillian to Jefferies, from Jefferies to Mansfield, they will not believe it possible that a learned judge can act in direct contradiction to those laws which he is supposed to have made the study of his life, and which he has sworn to administer faithfully. Superstition is certainly not the characteristic of this age. Yet some men are bigoted in politics who are infidels in religion. I do not despair of making them ashamed of their credulity.

The charge I brought against you is expressed in.

terms guarded and well considered. They do not deny the strict power of the judges of the court of king's bench to bail in cases, not bailable by a justice of peace, not replevisable by the common writ, or ex officio by the sheriff. I well know the practice of the court, and by what legal rules it ought to be directed. But, far from meaning to soften or diminish the force of those terms I have made use of, I now go beyond them, and affirm,

1. That the superior power of bailing for felony, claimed by the court of king's bench, is founded upon the opinion of lawyers, and the practice of the court; that the assent of the legislature to this power is merely negative; and that it is not supported by any positive provision in any statute whatsoever. If it be, produce the statute.

2. Admitting that the judges of the court of king's bench are vested with a discretionary power to examine and judge of circumstances and allegations, which a justice of peace is not permitted to consider, I affirm that the judges, in the use and application of that discretionary power, are as strictly bound by the spirit, intent, and meaning, as the justice of peace is by the words of the legislature.

Favourable circumstances, alledged before the judge, may justify a doubt whether the prisoner be guilty or not; and where the guilt is doubtful, a presumption of innocence should, in general, be admitted. But, when any such probable circumstances are alledged, they alter the state and condition of the prisoner. He is no longer that all-but-convicted felon, whom the law intends, and who by law is not bailable at all. If no circumstances whatsoever are alledged in his favour; if no allegation whatsoever be made to lessen the force of that evidence which the law annexes to a positive charge of felony, and particularly to the fact of 'being taken with the maner,' I then say that the lord chief justice of England has no more right to bail him than a justice of the peace. The discretion of an English judge is not of mere will and pleasure; it is not arbitrary; it is not capricious; but, as that great lawyer (whose authority I wish you respected half as much as I do) truly says, ' Discretion, taken as it ought to be, is, discernere ' per legem quid sit justum. If it be not directed by ' the right line of the law, it is a crooked cord, and ' appeareth to be unlawful.' If discretion were arbitrary in the judge, he might introduce whatever novelties he thought proper; but, says lord Coke, ' Novelties, without warrant of precedents, are not

' to be allowed; some certain rules are to be fol-
' lowed; Quicquid judicis authoritati subjicitur, no-
' vitati non subjicitur;' and this sound doctrine is
applied to the star-chamber, a court confessedly arbitrary. If you will abide by the authority of this great man, you shall have all the advantage of his opinion, wherever it appears to favour you. Excepting the plain express meaning of the legislature, to which all private opinions must give way, I desire no better judge between us than lord Coke.

3. I affirm that, according to the obvious, indisputable meaning of the legislature, repeatedly expressed, a person positively charged with feloniously stealing, and taken in flagrante delicto with the stolen goods upon him, is not bailable. The law considers him as differing in nothing from a convict but in the form of conviction, and (whatever a corrupt judge may do) will accept of no security but the confinement of his body within four walls. I know it has been alledged in your favour, that you have often bailed for murders, rapes, and other manifest crimes. Without questioning the fact, I shall not admit that you are to be justified by your own example. If that were a protection to you, where is the crime that, as a judge, you might not now securely commit? But

neither shall I suffer myself to be drawn aside from my present argument, nor you to profit by your own wrong. To prove the meaning and intent of the legislature will require a minute and tedious deduction. To investigate a question of law demands some labour and attention, though very little genius or sagacity. As a practical profession, the study of the law requires but a moderate portion of abilities. The learning of a pleader is usually upon a level with his integrity. The indiscriminate defence of right and wrong contracts the understanding, while it corrupts the heart. Subtlety is soon mistaken for wisdom, and impunity for virtue. If there be any instances upon record, as some there are undoubtedly, of genius and morality united in a lawyer, they are distinguished by their singularity, and operate as exceptions.

I must solicit the patience of my readers. This is no light matter, nor is it any more susceptible of ornament than the conduct of lord Mansfield is capable of aggravation.

As the law of bail, in charges of felony, has been exactly ascertained by acts of the legislature, it is at present of little consequence to inquire how it

stood at common law before the statute of Westminster. And yet it is worth the reader's attention to observe how nearly, in the ideas of our ancestors, the circumstance of ' being taken with the maner' approached to the conviction of the felon*. It ' fixed
' the authoritative stamp of verisimilitude upon the
' accusation, and by the common law, when a thief
' was taken with the maner (that is with the thing
' stolen upon him, in manu) he might, so detected
' flagrante delicto, be brought into court, arraigned,
' and tried, without indictment; as, by the Danish
' law, he might be taken and hanged upon the spot,
' without accusation or trial.' It will soon appear that our statute in law, in this behalf, though less summary in point of proceeding, is directed by the same spirit. In one instance, the very form is adhered to. In offences relating to the forest, if a man was taken with vert, or venison†, it was declared to be equivalent to indictment. To enable the reader to judge for himself, I shall state, in due order, the several statutes relative to bail in criminal cases, or as much of them as may be material to the point in question, omitting superfluous words. If I misre-

---

* Blackstone, iv. 303.

† 1 Ed. III. cap. 8.—and 7 Rich. II. cap. 4.

present or do not quote with fidelity, it will not be difficult to detect me.

The [u]statute of Westminster the first, in 1725, sets forth that, ' Forasmuch as sheriffs and others, ' who have taken and kept in prison persons detected ' of felony, and incontinent, have left out by re' plevin such as were not replevisable because they ' would gain of the one party and grieve the other; ' and, forasmuch as, before this time, it was not ' determined which persons were replevisable and ' which not, it is provided and by the king com' manded that such prisoners, &c. as be taken with ' the maner, &c. or for manifest offences, shall be ' in no wise replevisable by the common writ, nor ' without writ[x].' Lord Coke, in his exposition of the last part of this quotation, accurately distinguishes

---

[u] ' Videtur que le statute de main prise ne'est que rehersal del ' comen ley.'—Bro. Mainp. 61.

[x] ' There are three points to be considered in the construction ' of all remedial statutes; the old law, the mischief, and the re' medy; that is, how the common law stood at the making of the ' act, what the mischief was for which the common law did not ' provide, and what remedy the parliament hath provided to cure this ' mischief. It is the business of the judges so to construe the act, ' as to suppress the mischief and advance the remedy.'—Blackstone, i. 87.

between replevy by the common writ, or ex officio, and bail by the king's bench. The words of the statute certainly do not extend to the judges of that court. But, besides that the reader will soon find reason to think that the legislature, in their intention, made no difference between bailable and replevisable, Lord Coke himself (if he be understood to mean nothing but an exposition of the statute of Westminster, and not to state the law generally) does not adhere to his own distinction. In expounding the other offences which, by this statute, are declared 'not replevisable,' he constantly uses the words 'not bailable.' ' That outlaws, for instance, ' are not bailable at all; that persons, who have ab- ' jured the realm, are attainted upon their own con- ' fession, and therefore not bailable at all by law; ' that provers are not bailable; that notorious felons ' are not bailable.' The reason why the superior courts were not named in the statute of Westminster was plainly this, ' because anciently most of the bu- ' siness touching bailment of prisoners for felony ' or misdemeanors was performed by the sheriffs, or ' special bailiffs of liberties, either by writ, or virtute ' officii[y];' consequently the superior courts had little

[y] 2 Hale, P. C. 128. 136.

or no opportunity to commit those abuses which the statute imputes to the sheriffs. With submission to doctor Blackstone, I think he has fallen into a contradiction which, in terms at least, appears irreconcileable. After enumerating several offences not bailable, he asserts, without any condition or limitation whatsoever [z], ' all these are clearly not admis-
' sible to bail.' Yet in a few lines after he says,
' it is agreed that the court of king's bench may
' bail for any crime whatsoever, according to cir-
' cumstances of the case.' To his first proposition he should have added, ' by sheriffs or justices;' otherwise the two propositions contradict each other; with this difference, however, that the first is absolute, the second limited by a consideration of circumstances. I say this without the least intended disrespect to the learned author. His work is of public utility, and should not hastily be condemned.

The statute of 17 Richard II. cap. 10, 1393, sets forth, that ' forasmuch as thieves notoriously de-
' famed, and others taken with the maner, by their
' long abiding in prison, were delivered by charters,
' and favourable inquests procured, to the great hin-

---

[z] Blackstone, iv. 296.

'drance of the people, two men of law shall be
'assigned, in every commission of the peace, to
'proceed to the deliverance of such felons, &c.' It
seems by this act, that there was a constant struggle
between the legislature and the officers of justice.
Not daring to admit felons taken with the maner to
bail or mainprise, they evaded the law by keeping
the party in prison a long time, and then delivering
him without due trial.

The statute of 1 Richard III. in 1483, sets forth,
that 'forasmuch as divers persons have been daily
'arrested and imprisoned for suspicion of felony,
'sometime of malice, and sometime of a light sus-
'picion, and so kept in prison without bail or main-
'prise, be it ordained that every justice of peace shall
'have authority, by his discretion, to let such pri-
'soners and persons so arrested to bail or mainprise.'
By this act it appears that there had been abuses in
matter of imprisonment, and that the legislature
meant to provide for the immediate enlargement of
persons arrested on light suspicion of felony.

The statute of 3 Henry VII. in 1486, declares,
that 'under colour of the preceding act of Richard
'the Third, persons, such as were not mainperna-

' ble, were oftentimes let to bail or mainprise, by
' justices of the peace, whereby many murderers and
' felons escaped, the king, &c. hath ordained, that
' the justices of the peace, or two of them at least
' (whereof one to be of the quorum), have authority
' to let any such prisoners or persons, mainpernable
' by the law, to bail or mainprise.'

The statute of 1st and 2d of Philip and Mary, in 1554, sets forth, that ' notwithstanding the pre-
' ceding statute of Henry the Seventh, one justice
' of peace hath oftentimes, by sinister labour and
' means, set at large the greatest and notablest of-
' fenders, such as be not replevisable by the laws of
' this realm, and yet, the rather to hide their affec-
' tions in that behalf, have assigned the cause of
' their apprehension to be but only for suspicion of
' felony, whereby the said offenders have escaped
' unpunished, and do daily, to the high displeasure
' of Almighty God, the great peril of the king and
' queen's true subjects, and encouragement of all
' thieves and evil-doers; for reformation whereof be
' it enacted, that no justices of peace shall let to bail
' or mainprise any such persons which, for any of-
' fence by them committed, be declared not to be
' replevised, or bailed, or be forbidden to be reple-

' vised or bailed by the statute of Westminster the
' first; and furthermore that any persons arrested for
' manslaughter or felony, being bailable by the law,
' shall not be let to bail or mainprise, by any jus-
' tices of peace, but in the form therein after pre-
' scribed.' In the two preceding statutes, the words
bailable, replevisable, and mainpernable, are used
synonymously [a], or promiscuously, to express the
same single intention of the legislature, viz. ' not
' to accept of any security but the body of the of-
' fender;' and when the latter statute prescribes the
form in which persons arrested on suspicion of felony (being bailable by the law) may be let to bail,
it evidently supposes that there are some cases not
bailable by the law. It may be thought, perhaps,
that I attribute to the legislature an appearance of
inaccuracy in the use of terms, merely to serve my
present purpose. But, in truth, it would make more
forcibly for my argument to presume that the legislature were constantly aware of the strict legal distinction between bail and replevy, and that they
always meant to adhere to it [b]. For if it be true that

[a] 2 Hale, P. C. 2. 124.

[b] Vide 2 Inst. 150. 186.—' The word ' replevisable' signifies
' bailable.' ' Bailable is, in a court of record, by the king's justices;
' but replevisable is by the sheriff.' SELDEN, State Tr. vii. 149.

replevy is by the sheriffs, and bail by the higher courts at Westminster (which I think no lawyer will deny), it follows that, when the legislature expressly say, that any particular offence is by law not bailable, the superior courts are comprehended in the prohibition, and bound by it. Otherwise, unless there was a positive exception of the superior courts (which I affirm there never was in any statute relative to bail), the legislature would grossly contradict themselves, and the manifest intention of the law be evaded. It is an established rule that, when the law is special, and reason of it general, it is to be generally understood; and though, by custom, a latitude be allowed to the court of king's bench (to consider circumstances inductive of a doubt whether the prisoner be guilty or innocent), if this latitude be taken as an arbitrary power to bail, when no circumstances whatsoever are alledged in favour of the prisoner, it is a power without right, and a daring violation of the whole English law of bail.

The act of the 31st of Charles the Second (commonly called the habeas corpus act) particularly declares, that it is not meant to extend to treason or felony plainly and specially expressed in the warrant of commitment. The prisoner is therefore left to

seek his habeas corpus at common law; and so far was the legislature from supposing that persons (committed for treason or felony plainly and specially expressed in the warrant of commitment) could be let to bail by a single judge or by the whole court, that this very act provides a remedy for such persons in case they are not indicted in the course of the term or session subsequent to their commitment. The law neither suffers them to be enlarged before trial, nor to be imprisoned after the time, in which they ought regularly to be tried. In this case the law says, ' It shall and may be lawful
' to and for the judges of the court of king's bench
' and justices of oyer and terminer, or general gaol
' delivery, and they are hereby required, upon mo-
'. tion to them made in open court, the last day of
' the term, session, or gaol delivery, either by the
' prisoner or any one in his behalf, to set at liberty
' the prisoner upon bail; unless it appear to the
' judges and justices, upon oath made, that the wit-
' nesses for the king could not be produced the same
' term, sessions, or gaol delivery.' Upon the whole of this article I observe, 1. That the provision made in the first part of it, would be in a great measure useless and nugatory, if any single judge might have bailed the prisoner ex arbitrio during the vacation;

or if the court might have bailed him immediately after the commencement of the term or sessions. 2. When the law says, It shall and may be lawful to bail for felony under particular circumstances, we must presume that, before the passing of that act, it was not lawful to bail under those circumstances. The terms used by the legislature are enacting, not declaratory. 3. Notwithstanding the party may have been imprisoned during the greatest part of the vacation, and during the whole session, the court are expressly forbidden to bail him from that session to the next, if oath be made that the witnesses for the king could not be produced that same term or sessions.

Having faithfully stated the several acts of parliament relative to bail in criminal cases, it may be useful to the reader to take a short historical review of the law of bail, through its various gradations and improvements.

By the ancient common law, before and since the conquest, all felonies were bailable, till murder was excepted by statute, so that persons might be admitted to bail, before conviction, almost in every case. The statute of Westminster says that,

before that time, it had not been determined which offences were replevisable, and which were not, whether by the common writ de homine replegiando, or ex officio by the sheriff. It is very remarkable that the abuses arising from this unlimited power of replevy, dreadful as they were, and destructive to the peace of society, were not corrected or taken notice of by the legislature until the commons of the kingdom had obtained a share in it by their representatives; but the house of commons had scarce begun to exist, when these formidable abuses were corrected by the statute of Westminster. It is highly probable that the mischief had been severely felt by the people, although no remedy had been provided for it by the Norman kings or barons. ' The ini-
' quity of the times was so great, as it even forced
' the subjects to forego that which was in account a
' great liberty, to stop the course of a growing mis-
' chief.' The preamble to the statutes made by the first parliament of Edward the First, assigns the reason of calling it, ' because [d] the people had been
' otherwise entreated than they ought to be, the
' peace less kept, the laws less used, and offenders
' less punished, than they ought to be, by reason

[c] Seldon, by N. Bacon, 182.   [d] Parliamentary Hist. i. 52.

'whereof the people feared less to offend;' and the first attempt to reform these various abuses was by contracting the power of replevying felons.

For above two centuries following it does not appear that any alteration was made in the law of bail, except that being taken with vert or venison was declared to be equivalent to indictment. The legislature adhered firmly to the spirit of the statute of Westminster. The statute of 27th of Edward the First directs the justices of assize to inquire and punish officers bailing such as were not bailable. As for the judges of the superior courts, it is probable that, in those days, they thought themselves bound by the obvious intent and meaning of the legislature. They considered not so much to what particular persons the prohibition was addressed, as what the thing was which the legislature meant to prohibit, well knowing that in law, quando aliquid prohibetur, prohibetur et omne, per quod devenitur, ad illud. ' When any thing is forbidden, all the ' means by which the same thing may be compassed ' or done, are equally forbidden.'

By the statute of Richard the Third the power of bailing was a little enlarged. Every justice of peace was authorised to bail for felony; but they were expressly confined to persons arrested on light suspicion; and even this power, so limited, was found to produce such inconveniences that, in three years after, the legislature found it necessary to repeal it. Instead of trusting any longer to a single justice of peace, the act of 3 Henry VII. repeals the preceding act, and directs, ' that no prisoner (of those who ' are mainpernable by the law) shall be let to bail or ' mainprise, by less than two justices, whereof one ' to be of the quorum.' And so indispensably necessary was this provision thought for the administration of justice, and for the security and peace of society, that, at this time, an oath was proposed by the king to be taken by the knights and esquires of his household, by the members of the house of commons, and by the peers spiritual and temporal, and accepted and sworn to quasi unâ voce by them all, which, among other engagements, binds them ' not ' to let any man to bail or mainprise, knowing and ' deeming him to be a felon, upon your honour and ' worship. So help you God and all saints ^e.'

In about half a century, however, even these provisions were found insufficient. The act of Henry

^e Parliamentary History, ii. 519.

the Seventh was evaded, and the legislature once more obliged to interpose. The act of 1st and 2d of Philip and Mary takes away entirely from the justices all power of bailing for offences declared not bailable by the statute of Westminster.

The illegal imprisonment of several persons who had refused to contribute to a loan exacted by Charles the First, and the delay of the habeas corpus and subsequent refusal to bail them, constituted one of the first and most important grievances of that reign. Yet when the house of commons, which met in the year 1628, resolved upon measures of the most firm and strenuous resistance to the power of imprisonment assumed by the king or privy council, and to the refusal to bail the party on the return of the habeas corpus, they did expressly, in all their resolutions, make an exception of commitments where the cause of the restraint was expressed, and did by law justify the commitment. The reason of the distinction is, that, whereas when the cause of commitment is expressed, the crime is then known, and the offender must be brought to the ordinary trial; if, on the contrary, no cause of commitment be expressed, and the prisoner be thereupon remanded, it may operate to perpetual imprisonment. This contest with Charles the First produced the act of the 16th of that king, by which the court of king's bench are directed, within three days after the return to the habeas corpus, to examine and determine the legality of any commitment by the king or privy council, and to do what to justice shall appertain in delivering, bailing, or remanding the prisoner. Now, it seems, it is unnecessary for the judge to do what appertains to justice. The same scandalous traffic, in which we have seen the privilege of parliament exerted or relaxed, to gratify the present humour, or to serve the immediate purpose, of the crown, is introduced into the administration of justice. The magistrate, it seems, has now no rule to follow but the dictates of personal enmity, national partiality, or perhaps the most prostituted corruption.

To complete this historical inquiry, it only remains to be observed, that the habeas corpus act of the 31st of Charles the Second, so justly considered as another magna charta ᶠ of the kingdom, ' extends ' only to the case of commitments for such criminal ' charge as can produce no inconvenience to public ' justice by a temporary enlargement of the prisoner.'

ᶠ Blackstone, iv. 137.

So careful were the legislature, at the very moment when they were providing for the liberty of the subject, not to furnish any colour or pretence for violating or evading the established law of bail in the higher criminal offences. But the exception stated in the body of the act puts the matter out of all doubt. After directing the judges how they are to proceed to the discharge of the prisoner upon recognizance and surety, having regard to the quality of the prisoner and nature of the offence, it is expressly added, ' unless it shall appear to the said lord chan-
' cellor, &c. that the party so committed is detained
' for such matters, or offences, for the which, by
' the law, the prisoner is not bailable.'

When the laws, plain of themselves, are thus illustrated by facts, and their uniform meaning established by history, we do not want the authority of opinions, however respectable, to inform our judgment, or to confirm our belief. But I am determined that you shall have no escape. Authority of every sort shall be produced against you, from Jacob to lord Coke, from the dictionary to the classic. In vain shall you appeal from those upright judges whom you disdain to imitate, to those whom you have made your example. With one voice they all condemn you.

' To be taken with the maner is where a thief, ' having stolen any thing, is taken with the same ' about him, as it were in his hands, which is called ' flagrante delicto. Such a criminal is not bailable ' by law.—Jacob under the word Maner.

' Those who are taken with the maner are ex-' cluded by the statute of Westminster from the ' benefit of a replevin.'—Hawkins, P. C. 2. 98.

' Of such heinous offences no one who is noto-' riously guilty seems to be bailable by the intent of ' this statute.'—Ditto, 2. 99.

' The common practice and allowed general rule ' is, that bail is only then proper where it stands ' indifferent whether the party were guilty or inno-' cent.'—Ditto, ditto.

' There is no doubt but that the bailing of a '·person who is not bailable by law, is punishable ' either at common law as a negligent escape, or as

' an offence against the several statutes relative to
' bail.'—Ditto, 89.

' It cannot be doubted but that neither the judges
' of this, nor of any other superior court of justice,
' are strictly within the purview of that statute, yet
' they will always, in their discretion, pay a due re-
' gard to it, and not admit a person to bail who is
' expressly declared by it irreplevisable, without some
' particular circumstance in his favour; and there-
' fore it seems difficult to find an instance where per-
' sons attainted of felony, or notoriously guilty of
' treason or manslaughter, &c. by their own con-
' fession, or otherwise, have been admitted to the
' benefit of bail, without some special motive to the
' court to grant it.'—Ditto, 114.

' If it appears that any man hath injury or wrong
' by his imprisonment, we have power to deliver and
' discharge him; if otherwise, he is to be remanded
' by us to prison again.'—Lord ch. j. Hyde. State
Trials, 7. 115.

' The statute of Westminster was especially for
' direction to the sheriffs and others; but to say

' courts of justice are excluded from this statute, I
' conceive it cannot be.'—Attorney-general Heath,
Ditto, 132.

' The court upon view of the return, judgeth of
' the sufficiency or insufficiency of it. If they think
' the prisoner in law to be bailable, he is committed
' to the marshal, and bailed; if not, he is remand-
' ed.'—Through the whole debate the objection, on
the part of the prisoners, was, that no cause of commitment was expressed in the warrant; but it was
uniformly admitted by their counsel, that if the cause
of commitment had been expressed for treason or felony, the court would then have done right in remanding them.

The attorney-general having urged, before a com-
mittee of both houses, that, in Beckwith's case and
others, the lords of the council sent a letter to the
court of king's bench to bail, it was replied by the
managers of the house of commons, that this was
of no moment, ' for that either the prisoner was
' bailable by the law, or not bailable; if bailable by
' the law, then he was to be bailed without any
' such letter; if not bailable by the law, then plainly
' the judges could not have bailed him upon the let-

' ter, without breach of their oath, which is, that
' they are to do justice according to the law,' &c.—
State Trials, 7. 175.

' So that, in bailing upon such offences of the
' highest nature, a kind of discretion, rather than a
' constant law, hath been exercised, when it stands
' wholly indifferent in the eye of the court, whether
' the prisoner be guilty or not.'—Selden. State Tr.
7. 230. 1.

' I deny that a man is always bailable when im-
' prisonment is imposed upon him for custody.'—
Attorney-general Heath. ditto, 238.—By these quotations from the State Trials, though otherwise not
of authority, it appears plainly, that, in regard to
bailable or not bailable, all parties agreed in admit-
ing one proposition as incontrovertible.

' In relation to capital offences there are espe-
' cially these acts of parliament that are the common
' landmarks[s] touching offences bailable or not bail-
' able.' Hale 2 P. C. 127.—The enumeration in-
cludes the several acts cited in this paper.

[s] It has been the study of lord Mansfield to remove landmarks.

' Persons taken with the manouvre are not bail-
' able, because it is furtum manifestum.'—Hale 2.
P. C. 133.

' The writ of habeas corpus is of a high nature;
' for if persons be wrongfully committed, they are to
' be discharged upon this writ returned; or, if bail-
' able, they are to be bailed; if not bailable, they
' are to be committed.' Hale 2. P. C. 143.—This
doctrine of lord chief justice Hale refers immediately
to the superior courts from whence the writ issues.
' After the return is filed, the court is either to dis-
' charge, or bail, or commit him, as the nature of
' the case requires.' Hale 2. P. C. 146.

' If bail be granted otherwise than the law al-
' loweth, the party that alloweth the same shall be
' fined, imprisoned, render damages, or forfeit his
' place, as the case shall require.'— Selden by N.
Bacon. 182.

' This induces an absolute necessity of express-
' ing, upon every commitment, the reasons for which
' it is made; that the court, upon a habeas corpus,
' may examine into its validity, and, according to
' the circumstances of the case, may discharge, ad-

' mit to bail, or remand the prisoner.'—Blackstone. 3. 133.

' Marriot was committed for forging indorse-
' ments upon bank bills, and upon a habeas corpus
' was bailed, because the crime was only a great
' misdemeanor; for though forging the bills be fe-
' lony, yet forging the indorsement is not.'—Salkeld. 1. 104.

' Appell de Mahem, &c. ideo ne fuit lesse a
' baille, nient plus que in appell de robbery ou mur-
' der; quod nota, et que in robry et murder le partie
' n'est baillable.'—Bro. Mainprise. 67.

' The intendment of the law in bails is, quod
' stat indifferenter whether he be guilty or no; but
' when he is convicted by verdict or confession, then
' he must be deemed in law to be guilty of the fe-
' lony, and therefore not bailable at all.'—Coke.
2 Inst. 188.—4. 178.

' Bail is quando stat indifferenter, and not when
' the offence is open and manifest.'—2 Inst. 189.

' In this case non stat indifferenter whether he

' be guilty or no, being taken with the maner, that
' is, with the thing stolen, as it were in his hand.'—
Ditto, ditto.

' If it appeareth that this imprisonment be just
' and lawful, he shall be remanded to the former
' gaoler; but if it shall appear to the court that he
' was imprisoned against the law of the land, they
' ought, by force of this statute, to deliver him; if
' it be doubtful, and under consideration, he may
' be bailed.'— 2 Inst. 55.

It is unnecessary to load the reader with any farther quotations. If these authorities are not deemed sufficient to establish the doctrine maintained in this paper, it will be in vain to appeal to the evidence of law books, or to the opinions of judges. They are not the authorities by which lord Mansfield will abide. He assumes an arbitrary power of doing right; and if he does wrong, it lies only between God and his conscience.

Now, my lord, although I have great faith in the preceding argument, I will not say that every minute part of it is absolutely invulnerable. I am too well acquainted with the practice of a certain court, directed by your example, as it is governed by your authority, to think there ever yet was an argument, however conformable to law and reason, in which a cunning quibbling attorney might not discover a flaw. But, taking the whole of it together, I affirm that it constitutes a mass of demonstration, than which nothing more complete or satisfactory can be offered to the human mind. How an evasive, indirect reply will stand with your reputation, or how far it will answer in point of defence at the bar of the house of lords, is worth your consideration. If, after all that has been said, it should still be maintained, that the court of king's bench in bailing felons, are exempted from all legal rules whatsoever, and that the judge has no direction to pursue but his private affections, or more unquestionable will and pleasure, it will follow plainly, that the distinction between bailable and not bailable, uniformly expressed by the legislature, current through all our law books, and admitted by all our great lawyers without exception, is in one sense a nugatory, in another a pernicious distinction. It is nugatory, as it supposes a difference in the bailable quality of offences, when, in effect, the distinction refers only to the rank of the magistrate. It is pernicious, as it implies a rule of law which yet the judge is not bound to pay the least regard to, and impresses an idea upon the minds of the people, that the judge is wiser and greater than the law.

It remains only to apply the law, thus stated, to the fact in question. By an authentic copy of the mittimus, it appears that John Eyre was committed for felony, plainly and specially expressed in the warrant of commitment. He was charged before alderman Halifax by the oath of Thomas Fielding, William Holder, William Payne, and William Nash, for feloniously stealing eleven quires of writing paper, value six shillings, the property of Thomas Beach, &c. By the examinations upon oath, of the four persons mentioned in the mittimus, it was proved, that large quantities of paper had been missed, and that eleven quires (previously marked from a suspicion that Eyre was the thief) were found upon him. Many other quires of paper, marked in the same manner, were found at his lodgings; and after he had been some time in Wood-street compter, a key was found in his room there, which appeared to be a key to the closet at Guildhall, from whence the paper was stolen. When asked what he had to say in his defence, his only answer was, ' I hope you ' will bail me.' 'Mr. Holder, the clerk, replied,

' That is impossible. There never was an instance
' of it when the stolen goods were found upon the
' thief.' The lord mayor was then applied to, and
refused to bail him. Of all these circumstances it
was your duty to have informed yourself minutely.
The fact was remarkable, and the chief magistrate
of the city of London was known to have refused to
bail the offender. To justify your compliance with
the solicitations of your three countrymen, it should
be proved that such allegations were offered to you,
in behalf of their associate, as honestly and bona
fide reduced it to a matter of doubt and indifference
whether the prisoner was innocent or guilty. Was
any thing offered by the Scotch triumvirate that
tended to invalidate the positive charge made against
him by four credible witnesses upon oath? Was it
even insinuated to you, either by himself or his bail,
that no felony was committed; or that he was not
the felon; that the stolen goods were not found upon
him; or that he was only the receiver, not knowing
them to be stolen? Or, in short, did they attempt
to produce any evidence of his insanity? To all these
questions I answer for you, without the least fear of
contradiction, positively NO. From the moment he
was arrested he never entertained any hope of ac-
quittal, therefore thought of nothing but obtaining

bail, that he might have time to settle his affairs, convey his fortune into another country, and spend the remainder of his life in comfort and affluence abroad. In this prudential scheme of future happiness the lord chief justice of England most readily and heartily concurred. At sight of so much virtue in distress, your natural benevolence took the alarm. Such a man as Mr. Eyre, struggling with adversity, must always be an interesting scene to lord Mansfield. Or was it that liberal anxiety by which your whole life has been distinguished, to enlarge the liberty of the subject? My lord, we did not want this new instance of the liberality of your principles. We already knew what kind of subjects they were for whose liberty you were anxious. At all events, the public are much indebted to you for fixing a price at which felony may be committed with impunity. You bound a felon, notoriously worth thirty thousand pounds, in the sum of three hundred. With your natural turn to equity, and knowing, as you are, in the doctrine of precedents, you undoubtedly meant to settle the proportion between the fortune of the felon and the fine by which he may compound for his felony. The ratio now upon record, and transmitted to posterity under the auspices of lord Mansfield, is exactly one to a hundred. My lord, without intending it, you have laid a cruel restraint upon the genius of your countrymen. In the warmest indulgence of their passions they have an eye to the expence, and if their other virtues fail us, we have a resource in their economy.

By taking so trifling a security from John Eyre, you invited and manifestly exhorted him to escape. Although, in bailable cases, it be usual to take four securities, you left him in the custody of three Scotchmen, whom he might have easily satisfied for conniving at his retreat. That he did not make use of the opportunity you industriously gave him, neither justifies your conduct, nor can it be any way accounted for but by his excessive and monstrous avarice. Any other man but this bosom friend of three Scotchmen, would gladly have sacrificed a few hundred pounds, rather than submit to the infamy of pleading guilty in open court. It is possible indeed that he might have flattered himself, and not unreasonably, with the hopes of a pardon. That he would have been pardoned seems more than probable, if I had not directed the public attention to the leading step you took in favour of him. In the present gentle reign we well know what use has been made of the lenity of the court and of the mercy of the crown. The lord chief justice of England accepts of the hundredth part of the property of a felon taken in the fact, as a recognizance for his appearance. Your brother Smythe brow-beats a jury, and forces them to alter their verdict, by which they had found a Scotch serjeant guilty of murder; and though the Kennedies were convicted of a most deliberate and atrocious murder, they still had a claim to the royal mercy. They were saved by the chastity of their connexions. They had a sister; yet it was not her beauty, but the pliancy of her virtue, that recommended her to the king. The holy Author of our religion was seen in the company of sinners; but it was his gracious purpose to convert them from their sins. Another man, who in the ceremonies of our faith might give lessons to the great enemy of it, upon different principles keeps much the same company. He advertises for patients, collects all the diseases of the heart, and turns a royal palace into an hospital for incurables. A man of honour has no ticket of admission at St. James's. They receive him like a virgin at the Magdalen's; ' Go thou and ' do likewise.'

My charge against you is now made good. I shall however be ready to answer or to submit to fair objections. If, whenever this matter shall be agitated, you suffer the doors of the house of lords to be shut, I now protest, that I shall consider you as having made no reply. From that moment, in the opinion of the world, you will stand self-convicted. Whether your reply be quibbling and evasive, or liberal and in point, will be matter for the judgment of your peers; but if, when every possible idea of disrespect to that noble house (in whose honour and justice the nation implicitly confides) is here most solemnly disclaimed, you should endeavour to represent this charge as a contempt of their authority, and move their lordships to censure the publisher of this paper, I then affirm that you support injustice by violence, that you are guilty of a heinous aggravation of your offence, and that you contribute your utmost influence to promote, on the part of the highest court of judicature, a positive denial of justice to the nation.

JUNIUS.

Earl Camden.

LETTER LXIX.

TO

THE RIGHT HONOURABLE LORD CAMDEN.

MY LORD,

I TURN with pleasure from that barren waste in which no salutary plant takes root, no verdure quickens, to a character fertile, as I willingly believe, in every great and good qualification. I call you, in the name of the English nation, to stand forth in defence of the laws of your country, and to exert, in the cause of truth and justice, those great abilities with which you were intrusted for the benefit of mankind. To ascertain the facts set forth in the preceding paper, it may be necessary to call the persons mentioned in the mittimus to the bar of the house of lords. If a motion for that purpose should be rejected, we shall know what to think of lord Mansfield's innocence. The legal argument is submitted to your lordship's judgment. After the noble stand you made against lord Mansfield upon the question of libel, we did expect that you would not have suffered that matter to have remained undetermined. But it was said that lord chief justice Wilmot had been prevailed upon to vouch for an opinion of the late judge Yates, which was supposed to make against you; and we admit of the excuse. When such detestable arts are employed to prejudge a question of right, it might have been imprudent, at that time, to have brought it to a decision. In the present instance you will have no such opposition to contend with. If there be a judge, or a lawyer of any note in Westminster-hall, who shall be daring enough to affirm that, according to the true intendment of the laws of England, a felon, taken with the maner, in flagranti delicto, is bailable; or that the discretion of an English judge is merely arbitrary, and not governed by rules of law, I should be glad to be acquainted with him. Whoever he be, I will take care that he shall not give you much trouble.

Your lordship's character assures me that you will assume that principal part which belongs to you, in supporting the laws of England against a wicked judge, who makes it the occupation of his life to misinterpret and pervert them. If you decline this honourable office, I fear it will be said that, for some months past, you have kept too much company with the duke of Grafton. When the contest turns upon the interpretation of the laws, you cannot, without a formal surrender of all your reputation, yield the post of honour even to lord Chatham. Considering the situation and abilities of lord Mansfield, I do not scruple to affirm, with the most solemn appeal to God for my sincerity, that, in my judgment, he is the very worst and most dangerous man in the kingdom. Thus far I have done my duty in endeavouring to bring him to punishment. But mine is an inferior, ministerial office in the temple of justice. I have bound the victim, and dragged him to the altar.

JUNIUS.

The reverend Mr. John Horne having, with his usual veracity and honest industry, circulated a report that Junius, in a letter to the supporters of the bill of rights, had warmly declared himself in favour of long parliaments and rotten boroughs, it is thought necessary to submit to the public the following extract from his letter to John Wilkes, esq. dated the 7th of September 1771, and laid before the society on the 24th of the same month.

' With regard to the several articles, taken sepa-
' rately, I own I am concerned to see that the great
' condition, which ought to be the sine quâ non of
' parliamentary qualification, which ought to be the
' basis (as it assuredly will be the only support) of
' every barrier raised in defence of the constitution,
' I mean a declaration upon oath to shorten the
' duration of parliaments, is reduced to the fourth
' rank in the esteem of the society; and, even in
' that place, far from being insisted on with firm-
' ness and vehemence, seems to have been particu-
' larly slighted in the expression—" You shall en-

"deavour to restore annual parliaments!" Are these
'the terms which men who are in earnest make use
'of when the salus reipublicæ is at stake? I ex-
'pected other language from Mr. Wilkes. Besides
'my objection in point of form, I disapprove highly
'of the meaning of the fourth article as it stands.
'Whenever the question shall be seriously agitated,
'I will endeavour (and if I live will assuredly at-
'tempt it) to convince the English nation, by argu-
'ments to my understanding unanswerable, that
'they ought to insist upon a triennial, and banish
'the idea of an annual parliament...........
'I am convinced that, if shortening the duration of
'parliaments (which in effect is keeping the repre-
'sentative under the rod of the constituent) be not
'made the basis of our new parliamentary jurispru-
'dence, other checks or improvements signify no-
'thing. On the contrary, if this be made the foun-
'dation, other measures may come in aid, and, as
'auxiliaries, be of considerable advantage. Lord
'Chatham's project, for instance, of increasing the
'number of knights of shires, appears to me ad-
'mirable........ As to cutting away the rotten
'boroughs, I am as much offended as any man at
'seeing so many of them under the direct influence
'of the crown, or at the disposal of private persons.

'Yet, I own, I have both doubts and apprehensions
'in regard to the remedy you propose. I shall be
'charged perhaps with an unusual want of political
'intrepidity when I honestly confess to you, that I
'am startled at the idea of so extensive an amputa-
'tion. In the first place, I question the power, de
'jure, of the legislature to disfranchise a number of
'boroughs, upon the general ground of improving
'the constitution. There cannot be a doctrine more
'fatal to the liberty and property we are contending
'for, than that which confounds the idea of a su-
'preme and arbitrary legislature. I need not point
'out to you the fatal purposes to which it has been,
'and may be applied. If we are sincere in the po-
'litical creed we profess, there are many things
'which we ought to affirm cannot be done by king,
'lords, and commons. Among these I reckon the
'disfranchising of boroughs with a general view of
'improvement. I consider it as equivalent to rob-
'bing the parties concerned of their freehold, of their
'birthright. I say that, although this birthright
'may be forfeited, or the exercise of it suspended
'in particular cases, it cannot be taken away, by a
'general law, for any real or pretended purpose of
'improving the constitution. Supposing the at-
'tempt made, I am persuaded you cannot mean that

' either king, or lords, should take an active part in
' it. A bill, which only touches the representation
' of the people, must originate in the house of com-
' mons. In the formation and mode of passing it,
' the exclusive right of the commons must be as-
' serted as scrupulously as in the case of a money-
' bill. Now, sir, I should be glad to know by what
' kind of reasoning it can be proved that there is a
' power vested in the representative to destroy his
' immediate constituent. From whence could he
' possibly derive it? A courtier, I know, will be
' ready to maintain the affirmative. The doctrine
' suits him exactly, because it gives an unlimited
' operation to the influence of the crown. But we,
' Mr. Wilkes, ought to hold a different language.
' It is no answer to me to say, that the bill, when it
' passes the house of commons, is the act of the
' majority, and not the representatives of the parti-
' cular boroughs concerned. If the majority can dis-
' franchise ten boroughs, why not twenty, why not
' the whole kingdom? Why should not they make
' their own seats in parliament for life? When the
' septennial act passed, the legislature did what ap-
' parently and palpably they had no power to do;
' but they did more than people in general were

'aware of: they, in effect, disfranchised the whole 'kingdom for four years.

'For argument's sake, I will now suppose that
'the expediency of the measure, and the power of
'parliament, are unquestionable. Still you will
'find an insurmountable difficulty in the execution.
'When all your instruments of amputation are pre-
'pared, when the unhappy patient lies bound at your
'feet, without the possibility of resistance, by what
'infallible rule will you direct the operation? When
'you propose to cut away the rotten parts, can you
'tell us what parts are perfectly sound? Are there
'any certain limits, in fact or theory, to inform you
'at what point you must stop, at what point the
'mortification ends? To a man so capable of ob-
'servation and reflection as you are, it is unneces-
'sary to say all that might be said upon the subject.
'Besides that I approve highly of lord Chatham's
'idea of infusing a portion of new health into the
'constitution to enable it to bear its infirmities (a
'brilliant expression, and full of intrinsic wisdom),
'other reasons occur in persuading me to adopt it.
'I have no objection,' &c.

The man who fairly and completely answers this

argument, shall have my thanks and my applause. My heart is already with him. I am ready to be converted. I admire his morality, and would gladly subscribe to the articles of his faith. Grateful as I am to the GOOD BEING whose bounty has imparted to me this reasoning intellect, whatever it is, I hold myself proportionably indebted to him from whose enlightened understanding another ray of knowledge communicates to mine. But neither should I think the most exalted faculties of the human mind a gift worthy of the Divinity, nor any assistance in the improvement of them, a subject of gratitude to my fellow creature, if I were not satisfied, that really to inform the understanding corrects and enlarges the heart.

JUNIUS.

INDEX

TO THE

FIRST AND SECOND VOLUMES.

A.

AMERICA, Mr. Pitt and lord Camden the patrons of, vol. i. p. 8—a new office established for the business of, p. 9.

Army, young gentlemen coming into it said to be a security to the kingdom from foreign as well as domestic slavery, v. i. p. 34—many of our forces in climates unfavourable to British constitutions, p. 35—the insult offered to it by appointing colonel Luttrell adjutant general of Ireland, v. ii. p. 39.

B.

Beckford Mr. his sumptuous entertainment at the Mansion-house, v. ii. p. 149.

Bedford corporation of, admit strangers to their freedom, to shake off the tyranny of the duke of Bedford, v. i. p. 165 (note)—duke of, a letter to his grace from Junius, p. 160—his feelings nice, if to be judged from his resentments, ib.—what his grace was, and what he might have been, p. 162—his avowal of the sale of a borough, p. 165—accused of insensibility on the loss of his son, ib.—his grace every way unfortunate, p. 166—his embassy at Versailles the first important part of his history, p. 167—those who are acquainted with his grace's pecuniary character are apt to suspect such sacrifices would not have been made without some private compensations, ib.—stipulations made betwixt him and lord Bute, and violated, p. 168—behaves to the king in an outrageous manner, p. 169—solicits again the friendship of lord Bute, p. 170—his measures to obtain and confirm his power, ib.—his character vindicated by sir William Draper, p. 185—makes a public display of his insensibility on the death of his son, p. 193.

Benson Mr. challenged as a juryman, v. ii. p. 83.

Bingley Mr. his imprisonment for two years, v. ii. p. 49 (note).

Blackstone Dr. solicitor to the queen, v. i. p. 93—more solicitous to preserve his place than his reputation, ib.—a letter addressed to him from Junius, p. 120—charged with having delivered different doctrines in the house of commons from what he had written in his Commentaries, p. 126—that when he spoke in the house he never once thought of the Commentaries until the contradiction was unexpectedly urged, p. 130—contradicts the ministry sometimes as well as himself, p. 158.

Bradshaw Mr. affirms that every part of Mr. Hine's purchase money was paid to colonel Burgoyne, v. ii. p. 114 —an intimacy betwixt him and lord Irnham, 233 (note).

Bromfield Mr. surgeon, his opinion in regard to the death of George Clarke, who received a blow at the Brentford election, v. i. p. 54 (note).

Brooke Dr. said to be quartered on the salary of a patent place purchased by Mr. Hine, v. i. p. 230.

Bucarelli, the Spanish governor of Port Egmont, acted in obedience to his order, v. ii. p. 63—if he had acted without, he deserved death, p. 67.

Burgoyne colonel, his expences at Preston, v. i. p. 226— the purchase-money of a patent place said to be given him for his services. at Preston, p. 230—no man more tender of his reputation, p. 231.

Bute earl of, his interview with the duke of Bedford, v. i. p. 164 (note)—not of a temper to relinquish power, though he retired from employment, p. 168—stipulations made betwixt him and the duke of Bedford viovated, ib.—treats the duke with contempt when again soliciting his friendship, p. 170—forced into the prince of Wales's household, contrary to the late king's inclination, v. i. p. 237 (note).

C.

Calcraft Mr. when he determined to be a patriot, v. ii. p. 199.

Camden lord, attributes to the crown a power, in case of necessity, to suspend the operation of an act of the legislature, v. ii. p. 194—his doctrine in this respect considered and refuted, p. 204—a letter to his lordship from Junius, p. 275.

Carleton-house, the tutelage and dominion of the heir apparent laid there many years ago, v. i. p. 237 (note).

Charles I. lived and died a hypocrite, v. i. p. 78.

Charles II. a hypocrite, though of another sort, ib.

Chatham lord, introduces the duke of Grafton on the political stage, v. i. ib.—obliged to withdraw his name from an administration formed on the credit of it, p. 80 —the motive of giving the thanks of the city to him, v. ii. p. 150—an encomium on him by Junius, p. 160.

Clergy, their incapacity to sit in the house of commons, v. i. p. 136.

Coke sir Edward, his opinion with regard to the power of the house of commons committing for contempt, v. ii. p. 102.

Colonies, those of America alienated from their natural affection to the mother country, v. i. p. 8—receive spirit and argument from the declaration of Mr. Pitt and lord Camden, ib.—the stamp-act repealed, and a new mode of taxing the colonies invented, p. 9—the colonists equally detest the pageantry of a king and the hypocrisy of a bishop, p. 249.

Commons house of, the situation they are reduced to by

their vote on the Middlesex election, v. i. p. 147—said to have transferred their gratitude from their parents to their benefactors, p. 245—have assumed an authority equal to an act of the legislature, p. 255—have transferred the right of election from the collective to the representative body, p. 256—they are only interpreters to convey the sense of the people to the crown, v. ii. p. 19 —did not dare to assert their own dignity when grossly attacked, p. 28—would best consult their dignity by appealing to the laws, when they are offended, p. 91.

Corsica, would never have been invaded if the British court had interposed with dignity and firmness, v. i. p. 83.

Cromwell Oliver, with all his crimes, had the spirit of an Englishman, v. ii. p. 75—an expression of his in the time of Charles I. p. 144.

Cumberland the late duke of, in his time parliamentary influence prevailed least in the army, vol. i. p. 33.

D.

Dingley Mr. becomes a candidate for the county of Middlesex, v. i. p. 60 (note).

Dodd captain, applied to captain Garth for the assistance of his guard to rescue general Gansel, v. i. p. 217.

Draper sir William, his defence of the marquis of Granby against the charges of Junius, v. i. p. 16—his letter to Junius, p. 31—refers him to the united voice of the army, and all Germany, for instances of the military skill and capacity of the marquis of Granby, v. i. p. 33 —his answer on his own account, p. 36—accused of making a traffic of the royal favour, p. 43—another letter to Junius, p. 45—his answer to a question of Junius, ib.—to Junius, p. 175—complains of the assertion of Junius, that he had sold the companions of his success, ib.—that it is a malicious falsehood, and bids the writer stand forth and avow the charge, ib.—appeals to the gentlemen to whom he had made application in this affair, p. 177—to Junius, that he has read his letter to the duke of Bedford with horror and astonishment, wherein an affectionate father is upbraided with the loss of an only and most amiable son, p. 185—that Junius goes wantonly out of his way to torment declining age, ib — he is called upon to prove the duke's avarice before he makes his hasty and wicked conclusions, p. 187—but if an ambassador loves money too much, is this a proof that he has taken any to betray his country, ib.—sir William's account of the ministerial quarrels, p. 189—that the duke however, potent as he is, is amenable to justice, and the parliament is the high and solemn tribunal, p. 168.

E.

Ellis Mr. Welbore, whether he makes or suppresses a motion, is sure of his disgrace, v. ii. p. 14.

Expulsion from the house of commons, whether it creates incapacity of being re-elected, v. i. p. 132, et seq.— Mr. Walpole's case considered as a precedent, p. 137.

Eyre John, bailed by lord Mansfield, v. ii. p. 229—this affair stated and examined according to the statutes in such cases, p. 269.

F.

Felony, whether or not bailable, v. ii. p. 241—the statutes relative to bail in criminal matters stated in due order, p. 245.

Foote Mr. surgeon, his evidence on the trial of Mac Quirk, v. i. p. 54 (note).

G.

Game laws oppressive to the subject, v. ii. p. 226.

Gansel general, his rescue from the bailiffs near the Tiltyard in St. James's Park, v. i. p. 208—he solicited a corporal and other soldiers to assist him in making his escape, p. 217.

Garth captain, declined appearing himself, but stood aloof while captain Dodd took upon him to order out the king's guard to rescue general Gansel, v. i. p. 217.

Gisborne colonel, a regiment said to be sold to him, v. i. p. 29—colonel Draper resigned it to him for his halfpay, p. 39—accepts of a pension for the government of Kinsale, v. ii. p. 39.

Grafton duke of, upon what footing he first took, and

soon after resigned the office of secretary of state, v. i. p. 5 (note) — the only act of mercy to which he advised his sovereign received with disapprobation, p. 53 — his establishment of a new tribunal, p. 57 — one fatal mark fixed on every measure wherein he is concerned, p. 59 — a singular instance of youth without spirit, p. 61 — obliged either to abandon a useful partizan, or to protect a villain from public justice, p. 62 — accused of balancing his non-execution of the laws with a breach of the constitution, p. 69 — the seating Mr. Luttrell in the house of commons entails on posterity the immediate effects of his administration, ib. — in his system of government he addresses himself simply to the touch, p. 76 — his character considered as a subject of curious speculation, ib. — resemblance thereof to that of his royal progenitors, p. 78 — at his setting out, a patriot of no unpromising expectations, ib. — has many compensations to make in the closet for his former friendship with Mr. Wilkes, p. 79 — his union by marriage not imprudent in a political view, p. 81 — his grace's public conduct as a minister the counterpart of his private history, p. 82 — in the whole course of his life a strange endeavour to unite contradictions, ib. — his insult on public decorum at the opera-house, p. 94 — his reasons for deserting his friends, ib. — his political infant state, childhood, puberty, and manhood, p. 96 — if his grace's abilities had been able to keep pace with the principles of his heart, he would have been a formidable minister, v. i. p. 97—the people find a resource in the weakness of his understanding, ib.— charged with being the leader of a servile administration, collected from the deserters of all parties, p. 100—his coyness in rejecting Mr. Vaughan's proposals is said to resemble the termagant chastity of a prude, p. 225—is called upon to tell the price of the patent purchased by Mr. Hine, p. 226—will he dare (says Junius) to prosecute Vaughan whilst he is setting up the royal patronage to auction ? ib.—in his public character has injured every subject in the empire, p. 262—the event of all the sacrifices he made to lord Bute's patronage, ib.—at the most active period of life obliged to quit the busy scene, and conceal himself from the world, p. 263—the neglect of the petitions and remonstrances a part of his original plan of government, p. 265 —was contented with pronouncing colonel Luttrell's panegyric, v. ii. p. 38—is restored to his rank under the royal standard, p. 110—is acknowledged by Junius to have great intrinsic merit, but is cautioned not to value it too highly, p. 111—in vain would his majesty have looked round for a more consummate character, p. 112—he remembers with gratitude how the duke accommodated his morals to the necessity of his service, p. 113—the abundance of merit in the duke to secure the favour of his sovereign, p. 114—a striking peculiarity in his character, v. ii. p. 117—his grace's re-appointment in the cabinet announced to the public by the ominous return of lord Bute, p. 119 – in whatever measures concerned he makes the government of the best of princes contemptible and ridiculous, p. 120—his baseness affirmed to be the cause of greater mischief to England than even the unfortunate ambition of lord Bute, p. 162—to what enormous excesses the influence of the crown has conducted his grace without a spark of personal resolution, p. 175—in what a hopeful condition he delivered the navy to his successor, p. 179—the navy being in great want of timber, a warrant was made out to cut timber in Whittlebury forest, where the duke is hereditary ranger, ib.—his grace's persecution of the deputy-surveyor for attempting to cut down the trees when he happened not to have the warrant in his pocket, p. 180—the duke asserted upon his honour that in the grant the property of the timber is vested in the ranger, ib.—the very reverse affirmed to be the truth, p. 181—yet the oaks keep their ground, the king is defrauded, and the navy suffers; all this to appease the duke of Grafton, ib.— the mortification he received on the defeat of sir James Lowther, p. 231 —his expedition in hastening the grant to transfer the duke of Portland's property to sir James Lowther, p. 235.

Granby lord, accused of accumulating in his own person

and family a number of lucrative employments, v. i. p. 12—his cares confined to filling up vacancies, p. 13 —praised and vindicated by sir William Draper against the charge of Junius, p. 17—the united voice of the army and all Germany will tell instances of his military skill and capacity, p. 33—his reputation is said by Junius to have suffered more by his friends than his enemies, p. 41.

Grenville Mr. at any rate to be distressed because he was minister, v. i. p. 8—vindicated from some reflections thrown out against him in a pamphlet written in defence of sir William Blackstone, p. 121—receives chastisement from the chair in the house of commons, p. 130.

H.

Harley Mr. the interest of government in the city said to be committed to him, v. ii. p. 120.

Harry the eighth, by the submission of his parliament, as absolute as Lewis the fourteenth, v. ii. p. 75.

Hawke sir Edward, this country highly indebted to him, v. i. p. 13.

Hillsborough earl of, called forth to govern America, v. i. p. 9—his measures censured, ib.

Hine Mr. a patent purchased by him, v. i. p. 226—the price at which the place was knocked down, p. 230.

Horne Mr. his unfortunate endeavours in support of the nomination of sheriffs, v. ii. p. 122—in his principles already a bishop, v. ii. p. 122—his letter to Junius, p. 124 —'tis the reputation gained under this signature which draws from him a reply, p. 125—that he is ready to lay down his life in opposition to the ministerial measures, ib.—that he did not solicit one vote in favour of Messrs. Plumbe and Kirkman, p. 126—a letter to him from Junius, p, 128—accused of having sold himself to the ministry, from his own letters, ib.—his mode of attack on Mr. Wilkes censured, p. 130—is blamed for introducing the name of a young lady into the newspapers, p. 131—is charged with having duped Mr. Oliver, ib.—another letter to Junius, p. 133—charges him with inconsistency and self contradiction, p. 134—that he feels no reluctance to attack the character of any man, p. 137—that the darkness in which Junius thinks himself shrouded has not concealed him, p. 141—reflections on the tendency of Junius's principles, p. 145—that Mr. Wilkes did commission Mr. Thomas Walpole to solicit a pension for him, p. 146—that according to Junius Mr. Wilkes ought to hold the strings of his benefactors' purses ' so long as he continues to be a thorn in the king's side,' p. 148—that the leaders of the opposition refused to stipulate certain points for the public in case they should get into administration, p. 149—a letter from Mr. Horne to Junius, p. 153—is charged with changing the terms of Junius's proposition when he supposes him to assert it would be impossible for any man to write in the newspapers, and not to be discovered, v. ii. p. 155—that he deals in fiction, and therefore naturally appeals to the evidence of the poets, p. 157—is allowed a degree of merit which aggravates his guilt, ib.—his furious persecuting zeal has by gentle degrees softened into moderation, p. 159 —shameful for him who has lived in friendship with Mr. Wilkes to reproach him for failings naturally connected with despair, p. 163.

Humphrey Mr. his treatment of the duke of Bedford on the course at Litchfield, v. i. p. 166 (note).

I.

Ireland the people of, have been uniformly plundered and oppressed, v. i. p. 248.

Irnham lord, father of colonel Luttrell, v. ii. p. 233 (note).

Judge, one may be honest enough in the decision of private causes, yet a traitor to the public, v. i. p. 13.

Junius, letter from, to the printer of the Public Advertiser, on the state of the nation, and the different departments of the state, v. i. p. 1—to sir William Draper, p. 23— approves of sir William's spirit in giving his name to the public, but that it was a proof of nothing but spirit, p. 24—requires some instances of the military skill and capacity of lord Granby, p. 25—puts some queries to sir William as to his own conduct, p. 26—called upon by sir William to give his real name, p. 31'—another letter to sir William Draper, p. 41—explains sir William's bargain with colonel Gisborne, v. i. p. 43—letter to sir William Draper, p. 47—declares himself to be a plain unlettered man, p. 48—calls upon sir William to justify his declaration of the sovereign's having done an act in his favour contrary to law, p. 49—takes his leave of sir William, p. 50—letter to the duke of Grafton, p. 52—that the only act of mercy to which the duke advised his majesty meets with disapprobation, p. 53— that it was hazarding too much to interpose the strength of prerogative between such a felon as Mac Quirk, and the justice of his country, p. 54—the pardoning of this man, and the reasons alledged for so doing, considered, p. 57—to the duke of Grafton, p. 59—that one fatal mark seems to be fixed on every measure of his grace, whether in a personal or political character, ib.—that a certain ministerial writer does not defend the minister as to the pardoning Mac Quirk upon his own principles, p. 61—that his grace can best tell for which of Mr. Wilkes's good qualities he first honoured him with his friendship, p. 62—to Mr. Edward Weston, p. 64— a citation from his pamphlet in defence of the pardoning of Mac Quirk, with remarks, p. 65—to the duke of Grafton, p. 67—that his grace was at first scrupulous of even exercising those powers with which the executive power of the legislature is invested, ib.—that he reserved the proofs of his intrepid spirit for trials of greater hazard, p. 68—that he balanced the non-execu-

tion of the laws with a breach of the constitution, v. i.
p. 69—to the duke of Grafton, p. 75—that his grace
addresses himself simply to the touch, p. 76—his character resembles that of his royal ancestors, p. 78—to
the duke of Grafton, p. 97—if his grace's talents could
keep pace with the principles of his heart he would
have been a most formidable minister, ib.— that he
became the leader of an administration collected from
the deserters of all parties, p. 100—to the printer of the
Public Advertiser, p. 107—the question arising from
Mr. Wilkes's expulsion, and the appointment of Mr.
Luttrell attempted to be stated with justice and precision, ib.—the expulsion of Mr. Walpole, and his reelection, how far a case in point, p. 111—to sir William
Blackstone, p. 120—a certain pamphlet written in defence of sir William's conduct, considered, ib.— Mr.
Grenville and sir William Meredith vindicated from
some aspersions in this pamphlet, p. 122—that a certain
writer who defends the proceedings with regard to the
Middlesex election only quotes such parts of Mr. Walpole's case as seems to suit his purpose, p. 143—that
the house meant to declare Mr. Walpole's incapacity
arose from the crimes he had committed, p. 145—they
also declared the other candidate not duly elected,
p. 147—explanation of some passages in the last letter,
p. 152—to the duke of Bedford, p. 161—that he has
lost much real authority and importance, p. 162—the

degree of judgment he has shewn in carrying his own system into execution, v. i. p. 166—the importance of his embassy to the court of Versailles, p. 167—the measures he took to obtain and confirm his power, p. 171 —to sir William Draper, p. 179—that after having attacked Junius under that character he had no right to know him under any other, p. 180—that sir William was appointed colonel to a regiment greatly out of his turn, p. 181—Junius thinks it by no means necessary that he should be exposed to the resentment of the worst and most powerful men in this country, p. 182. —to sir William Draper, p. 191—sir William still continues to be a fatal friend, p. 192—he considers nothing in the cause he adopts but the difficulty of defending it, ib.—he may rest assured the duke of Bedford laughs with equal indifference at Junius's reproaches and sir William's distress about him, p. 193—admitting the single instance of his grace's generosity, the public may perhaps demand some other proofs of his munificence, p. 194—though there was no document left of any treasonable negociation, yet the conduct and known temper of the minister carried an internal evidence, p. 195—to the printer of the Public Advertiser, p. 198—Junius applauds the spirit with which a lady has paid the debt of gratitude to her benefactor, ib.— this single benevolent action is perhaps the more conspicuous from standing alone, ib.—to the printer of the

Public Advertiser, v. i. p. 206—the present ministry singularly marked by their fortunes as their crimes, ib.—they seem determined to perplex us with the multitude of their offences, p. 207—a major-general of the army arrested for a considerable debt, and rescued by a serjeant and some private soldiers, p. 208—that this is a wound given to the law, and no remedy applied, p. 209—the main question is, how the ministry have acted on this occasion, p. 210—the aggravating circumstances of this affair, p. 211—that the regiments of guards as a corps are neither good subjects nor good soldiers, p. 212—the marching regiments the bravest troops in the world, ib.—to the printer of the Public Advertiser, p. 222—that he admits the claim of Modestus in the Gazetteer, ib.—that Modestus having insinuated that the offenders in the rescue may still be brought to a trial, any attempt to prejudge the cause would be highly improper, ib—if the gentlemen, whose conduct is in question, are not brought to a trial, the duke of Grafton shall hear from him again, p. 223— leaves it to his countrymen to determine whether he is moved by malevolence, or animated by a just purpose of obtaining a satisfaction to the laws of the country, ib.—to his grace the duke of Grafton, p. 225—Junius gives his grace credit for his discretion in refusing Mr. Vaughan's proposals, ib—asks what was the price of Mr. Hine's patent, p. 226—and whether the duke dares to complain of an attack upon his own honour while he is selling the favours of the crown, v. i. p. 226—to his grace the duke of Grafton, p. 228—Junius is surprised at the silence of his grace's friends to the charge of having sold a patent place, p. 230—the price at which the place was knocked down, ib.—that there is none of all his grace's friends hardy enough to deny the charge, p. 232—that Mr. Vaughan's offer amounted to a high misdemeanor, p. 233—the opinion of a learned judge on this matter, ib.—to the printer of the Public Advertiser, p. 235—Junius supposes a well-intentioned prince asking advice for the happiness of his subjects, ib.—and an honest man when permitted to approach a king in what terms he would address himself to his sovereign, p. 236—he separates the amiable prince from the folly and treachery of his servants, p. 238—and that the king should distinguish between his own dignity, and what serves only to promote the interest and ambition of a minister, ibid.—that he should withdraw his confidence from all parties, and consult his own understanding, p. 239—that there is an original bias in his education, p. 240—that a little personal motive of pique was sufficient to remove the ablest servants of the crown, ib.—that Mr. Wilkes, though he attacked the favourite, was unworthy of a king's personal resentment, p. 243—that the destruction of one man has been for years the sole object of government,

v. i. p. 243—that his ministers have forced the subjects from wishing well to the cause of one man to unite with him in their own, p. 245—that nothing less than a repeal of a certain resolution can heal the wound given to the constitution, ib.—if an English king be hated or despised, he must be unhappy, p. 247—that the prince takes the sense of the army from the conduct of the guards, as he does that of the people from the representations of the ministry, p. 252—that the house of commons have attributed to their own vote an authority equal to an act of the legislature, p. 255—to the duke of Grafton, p. 261—in his public character he has injured every subject of the empire, p. 262—at the most active period of life he must quit the busy scene, and conceal himself from the world, p. 263—that the neglect of the remonstrances and petitions was part of his original plan of government, p. 265—the situation in which he abandoned his royal master, p. 266—that he either differed from his colleagues, or thought the administration no longer tenable, p. 268—that he began with betraying the people, and concluded with betraying the king, p. 269—Junius takes leave of the duke, p. 272—to the printer of the Public Advertiser, v. ii. p. 1—the king's answer to the city remonstrance considered, p. 2—the grievances of the people aggravated by insults, ib.—if any part of the representative body be not chosen by the people, that part vitiates and corrupts the whole, v. ii. p. 4—instead of an answer to the petition his majesty pronounces his own panegyric, p. 5—whether the remonstrance be or be not injurious to the parliament, is the very question between the parliament and the people, p. 6—the city of London has not desired the king to assume a power placed in other hands, p. 7—they call upon him to make use of his royal prerogative, p. 8—to the printer of the Public Advertiser, p. 9—that the king's answer to the city remonstrance is only the sentiments of the minister, ib.—the consequences however materially affect his majesty's honour, p. 10—he should never appear but in an amiable light to his subjects, p. 11—his majesty introduced too often in the present reign to act for or defend his servants, p. 15—an appeal to his majesty's judgment, p. 16—addresses from parliament considered as a fashionable unmeaning formality, p. 17.—the consequences of them considered when supposed to mean what they profess, ib.—to the printer of the Public Advertiser, p. 20—while parliament was sitting, it would neither have been safe nor regular to offer any opinion concerning their proceedings, ib.—we had a right to expect something from their prudence, and something from their fears, p. 21—the majority of the house of lords join with the other house, p. 26—they would hardly have yielded so much to the other house without the certainty of a compensation, p. 27—the house of commons did not vindicate their own dignity when grossly attacked, v. ii. p. 28—the business of the session after voting the supplies and settling the Middlesex election, p. 30—the situation of the king after the prorogation of parliament, p. 32—to lord North, p. 37—the honour of rewarding Mr. Luttrell's services reserved for his lordship, ib.—is called upon to tell who advised the king to appoint colonel Luttrell adjutant-general to the army of Ireland, p. 39—some secret purpose in view by such an appointment, p. 40—to lord Mansfield, p. 42—the danger of writing to his lordship, as he becomes party and judge, p. 43—a tribute paid to his Scotch sincerity, ib.—that he consoles himself for the loss of a favourite family by reviving the maxims of their government, p. 45—that his maxims of jurisprudence direct his interpretation of the laws and treatment of juries, ib.—that the court of king's bench becomes thereby a court of equity, p. 47—his conduct with regard to Bingley's affair, p. 48—that he invades the province of a jury in the matter of libel, p. 49—that his charge to the jury in the prosecution against Almon and Woodfall contradicted the highest legal authorities, p. 51—that he ordered a special juryman to be set aside without any legal objection, p. 53—is accused of having done great mischiefs to this country as a minister, p. 54—to the printer of the Public Advertiser, p. 60—violence and oppression at home supported by treachery and submission abroad, v. ii. p. 60—the plan of domestic policy from his majesty's accession to the throne engrosses all the attention of his servants, ib.—the expedition of the Spaniards against Port Egmont, p. 62—his majesty's ship detained in port above twenty days, ib.—the king's speech, Nov. 1770, considered, p. 63—if the actual situation of Europe be considered, when the affair of Port Egmont happened, the treachery of the king's servants must appear in the strongest colours, p. 68—a most favourable opportunity lost, ib.—the materials of a fable from the affair of Port Egmont, p. 70—to the printer of the Public Advertiser, p. 78—nothing now to be apprehended from prerogative, but much from undue influence, p. 81— our political climate severely altered, p. 83—the nature and origin of privileges traced and considered, p. 84— to the printer of the Public Advertiser, p. 104—an extract from the journals of the house of commons, p. 105 —a question or two put thereupon to the advocates for privilege, p. 106—to the duke of Grafton, p. 110— that his majesty would in vain have looked round the kingdom for a character so consummate as his grace's, p. 112—that his grace did not neglect the magistrate while he flattered the man, p. 113—that he has merit in abundance to recommend him to the sovereign, p. 114 —that he has never formed a friendship which has not been fatal to the object of it, p. 117—the services he has done his master have been faithfully recorded, v. ii. p. 119—his grace's reappointment to a seat in the cabibinet, how announced to the public, ib.—the duke is the pillow on which Junius proposes to rest all his resentments, p. 122—to the Rev. Mr. Horne, p. 128— from Mr. Horne's own letters he is supposed to have sold himself to the ministry, ib.—in order to gratify his personal hatred to Mr. Wilkes, that he sacrificed the cause of the country as far as was in his power, p. 129—when the public expected discoveries highly interesting to the community from Mr. Horne, what a pitiful detail was produced, p. 130—he has so little power to do mischief that it is much to be questioned if the ministry will adhere to the promises they may have made him, p. 131— to the printer of the Public Advertiser, p. 153—if any coarse expressions have escaped Junius, he agrees they are unfit for his pen, but that they may not have been improperly applied, p. 154—upon Mr. Horne's terms there is no danger in being a patriot, p. 158—by what gentle degrees his persecuting zeal has softened into moderation, p. 159—an high encomium on lord Chatham, p. 160—what excuse can Mr. Horne make for labouring to promote such a consummately bad man as Mr. Wilkes to a station of such trust and importance, p. 164—the best of princes not displeased with the abuse thrown upon his ostensible ministers, p. 166—to the duke of Grafton, p. 174—that he has done as much mischief to the community as Cromwell would have done had he been a coward, v. ii. p. 175—the enormous excesses through which court influence has safely conducted his grace without a ray of real understanding, ib.—it is like the universal passport of an ambassador, ib.—his majesty in want of money, and the navy in want of timber, p. 178—a warrant made out for cutting down any trees in Whittlebury forest, of which the duke is hereditary ranger, p. 179—his grace's behaviour on this occasion, p 180—to the livery of London, p. 184—that the election of their chief magistrate was a point in which every member of the community was interested, p. 185—the question to those who mean fairly to the liberty of the people lies within a very narrow compass, ib.—Mr. Nash's character considered as a magistrate and a public man, p. 186—he cannot alter his conduct, without confessing that he never acted upon principle of any kind, ib.—to the printer of the Public Advertiser, p. 186—Junius laments the unhappy differences which have arisen among the friends of the people, ib.—the insidious partizan who foments the disorder, sees the fruit of his industry ripen beyond his hopes, ib.—that Mr. Wilkes has no resource but in the public favour, p. 191—that Mr. Sawbridge has shewn himself possessed of that republican firmness which the times require, p. 192—the right of pressing founded originally upon a necessity which supersedes all argument, v. ii. p. 195—the designs of lord Mansfield subtle, effectual, and secure, p. 197—we should not reject the services or friendship of any man because he differs from us in a particular opinion, p. 198—patriotism, it seems, may be improved by transplanting, p. 199—Junius defended in three material points, p. 223 —charges lord Mansfield with doing what was illegal in bailing Eyre, p. 228—to the duke of Grafton, p. 231—the miserable depression of his grace when almost every man in the kingdom was exulting in the defeat of sir James Lowther, ib.—that he violates his own rules of decorum when he does not insult the man whom he has betrayed, p. 232—to lord chief justice Mansfield — Junius undertakes to prove the charge against his lordship, p. 238—that the superior power of bailing for felony claimed by the court of king's bench has only the negative assent of the legislature, p. 241— that a person positively charged with feloniously stealing, and taken with the stolen goods upon him, is not bailable, p. 243—authorities quoted to support this opinion, p. 246—the several statutes relative to bail in criminal cases stated in due order, ib.—the law as stated applied to the case of John Eyre, who was committed for felony, p. 269—to the right hon. lord Camden, p. 275—Junius calls upon his lordship to stand forth in defence of the laws of his country, ib.—extract of a letter from Junius to Mr. Wilkes, p. 278.

L.

Ligonier lord, the army taken from him much against his inclination, v. i. p. 28.

London city of, has given an example in what manner a king of this country should be addressed, v. i. p. 104.

Lottery, the worst way of raising money upon the people, v. i. p. 7.

Loyalty, what it is, v. i. p. 2.

Luttrell Mr. patronized by the duke of Grafton with success, v. i. p. 69—the assertion that two-thirds of the nation approve of his admission into parliament cannot be maintained nor confuted by argument, p. 92 – the appointment of, invades the foundations of the laws themselves, p. 102.

Lynn burgesses of, re-elect Mr. Walpole after being expelled, v. i. p. 111.

M.

Macquirk, the king's warrant for his pardon, v. i. p. 54 (note)—the pardoning of him much blamed, and the reasons alleged for so doing refuted, p. 57.

Manilla ransom, dishonourably given up, v. i. p. 25—the ministers said to be desirous to do justice in this affair, but their efforts in vain, p. 37.

Mansfield lord, extracts from his speech in the court of king's bench, in regard to the offer of money made by Vaughan to the duke of Grafton for the reversion of a place, v. i. p. 228 (note)—a tribute paid by Junius to his Scotch sincerity, v. ii. p. 43—that his lordship had some original attachments which he took every opportunity to acknowledge, ib.—is charged with reviving the maxims of government of his favourite family, p. 45—that he follows an uniform plan to enlarge the power of the crown, ib.—that he labours to contract the power of the jury, p. 46—that instead of positive rules by which a court should be determined, he has introduced his own unsettled notions of equity, p. 47—his conduct in regard to Bingley's confinement and release, p. 48—his charge to the jury in cases of libel contradicts the highest legal authorities, p. 51—his lordship reminded of the name of Benson, p. 53—charged with doing much mischief to this country as a minister, p. 54—the suspicious applause given by him to lord Chatham, p. 208—the doctrine he delivers to a jury, ib.—his reasons for challenging a juryman, p. 210—accused of endeavouring to screen the king's brother, p. 211—charged by Junius for bailing a man not bailable by the laws of England, p. 243.

Middlesex the election for, attended with one favourable consequence for the people, v. i. p. 71—the question in this affair is, whether by the law of parliament expulsion alone creates a disqualification, v. ii. p. 96—as a fact highly injurious to the rights of the people, and as a precedent one of the most dangerous, p. 99.

Ministers, to be acquainted with the merit of, we need

only observe the conduct of the people, v. i. p. 3—the misconduct of, has produced a sudden and extraordinary change within these few years in Great Britain, p. 4—the conduct and character, not the description of ministers, the cause of national calamities, p. 24—the minister who by corruption invades the freedom of election, and the ruffian who by open violence destroys that freedom, embarked in the same bottom, p. 54—he is the tenant of the day, and has no interest in the inheritance, v. ii. p. 18.

Modestus, charges Junius with absurdity in his writings, v. i. p. 200—cannot distinguish between a sarcasm and a contradiction, ib.—is accused of misquoting what Junius says of conscience, and making the sentence ridiculous by making it his own, p. 201.

Musgrave Dr. his firmness and integrity on his examination before the house of commons, v. ii. p. 28 (note).

N.

Nash Mr. his behaviour as a magistrate and a public man considered, v. ii. p. 186.

Nation, when the safety of it is at stake, suspicion is a sufficient ground for inquiry, v. i. p. 3.

North lord, chancellor of the exchequer, v. i. p. 6—is warned to think seriously before he increases the public debt, ib.—his boasted firmness and consistency, v. ii. p. 14.—had the means in his possession of reducing all the four per cents at once, v. ii. p. 31—had the honour of rewarding Mr. Luttrell's services, p. 37—is called upon by Junius to tell who advised the king to appoint colonel Luttrell adjutant-general of the army of Ireland, p. 39—that he shall not have time to new model the Irish army, p. 41—perhaps only the blind instrument of lord Bute and the princess dowager, ib.

Noye Mr. attorney-general, his opinion of the privilege of the house of commons to commit for contempt, v. ii. p. 101.

O.

Old Noll destined to be the ruin of the house of Stuart, v. i. p. 91—does not deny that Corsica has been sacrificed to the French, p. 95.

P.

Parsons Ann, mistress to the duke of Grafton, v. i. p. 73 (note)—led into public by his grace, and placed at the head of his table, p. 88—handed through the opera-house in presence of the queen by the first lord of the treasury, p. 94.

Parties, the idea of uniting does not produce the salutary effects intended thereby, v. i. p. 4.

People, submission of a free one, a compliance with laws which they themselves have enacted, v. i. p. 1—in reading the history of, how we become interested in their cause, p. 2 — an impartial administration of justice the firmest bond to engage their affections to government, v. i. p. 13.

Percy earl, placed at the head of a regiment, v. i. p. 34—aid-de-camp to the king, and had the rank of colonel before he had the regiment, p. 42.

Philo-Junius to the printer of the Public Advertiser, v. i. p. 87—that the duke of Grafton's friends, in the contest with Junius, are reduced to the general charge of scurrility and falsehood—the truth of Junius's facts of importance to the public, ib.—a revisal and consideration of them as they appeared in letter 12—another letter of his to the printer of the Public Advertiser, p. 91—that in the whole course of the duke of Grafton's life there is a strange endeavour to unite contradictions, ib. —a violation of public decorum should never be forgiven, p. 93—the duke of Grafton's conduct in this respect, p. 94—his grace has always some reason for deserting his friends, ib.—to the printer of the Public Advertiser, p. 115—the objections of G. A. to Junius's state of the question as to the Middlesex election considered, ib.—to the printer of the Public Advertiser, p. 129—that a correspondent of the St. James's Evening Post misunderstood Junius, ib. — that it appears evident that Dr. Blackstone never once thought of his commentaries when speaking in the house of commons, until the contradiction was urged, p. 130—charges the ministry with introducing a new system of logic, which he calls argument against fact, v. i. p. 150—to the printer of the Public Advertiser, p. 199—that he is assured Junius will never descend to a dispute with such a writer as Modestus, ib.—an examination of the instances brought to support the charge of Junius being an Irishman, p. 200, &c.—that Modestus misquotes what Junius says of conscience, and makes the sentence ridiculous by making it his own, p. 203—that Anti-Junius triumphs in having, as he supposes, cut off an out-post of Junius, v. ii. p. 73—that Junius does not speak of the Spanish nation, but the Spanish court, as the natural enemies of England, ib.—if it were not the respect he bears the minister he could name a man, who, without one grain of understanding, can do half as much as Oliver Cromwell, p. 75—as to a secret system in the closet, that this can only be determined by appearances, p. 76—the queries put by Anti-Junius can be only answered by the ministry, ib.— to the printer of the Public Advertiser, p. 94 — that those who object to detached parts of Junius's last letter do not mean fairly, or have not considered the scope of his argument, ib.—that Junius does not expect a dissolution of parliament will destroy corruption, but will be a terror and check to their successors, ib.—to the printer of the Public Advertiser, p. 96—Junius's construction of the vote, declaring Mr. Walpole's incapacity, ib.—a quotation from a tract of Lord Sommers to support this construction, v. ii. p. 97—if this construction be admitted, the advocates of the house of commons must be reduced to the necessity of maintaining one of the grossest absurdities, p. 98—that the house of commons certainly did not foresee one effect proceeding from their vote about the Middlesex election, p. 99—to the printer of the Public Advertiser, p. 168—the vanity and impiety of Junius are become the perpetual topics of abuse, ib.—the proofs brought to support such charges considered, p. 169—the charge of vanity and impiety proved to destroy itself, ib.—to the printer of the Public Advertiser, p. 203—that Junius's inclination leads him to treat lord Camden with particular respect and candour, ib.—that his lordship overshot himself in asserting the proclamation against exporting corn was legal, p. 205—to Zeno, p. 207—that the sophistry of this author's letter in defence of lord Mansfield is adapted to the character he defends, ib.—the suspicious applause given by his lordship to the man he detests, p. 208—his doctrine as delivered to a jury, ib.—his challenging a juryman, p. 210—is accused of endeavouring to screen the king's brother, p. 211—and incessantly labouring to introduce new modes of proceeding in the court where he presides, ib.—to an Advocate in the Cause of the People, p. 216—the difference between general warrants and press-warrants stated and explained, ib.

S.

Sawbridge Mr. has shewn himself possessed of that republican firmness which the times require, v. ii. p. 192.

Shelburne lord, applied to in regard to the Manilla ransom, v. i. p. 37.

Stamp-act made and repealed, v. i. p. 9.

Starling Solomon, apothecary, his opinion in regard to the death of Clarke, who received a blow at the Brentford election, vol. i. p. 54 (note).

State, the principal departments of, when improperly bestowed the cause of every mischief, v. i. p. 5.

T.

Townshend Mr. complains that the public gratitude has not been equal to his deserts, v. ii. p. 193.

Touchet Mr. in his most prosperous fortune, the same man as at present, v. ii. p. 120.

V.

Vaughan Mr. sends proposals to the duke of Grafton, v. i. p. 225—his offers to the duke amounted to a high misdemeanor, p. 233—a prosecution commenced against him, p. 228 (note)—the matter solemnly argued in the court of king's bench, ib.—Junius does justice to this injured man, p. 303.

W.

Weston Edward, a letter to him from Junius, v. i. p. 64 —quotations from his pamphlet, in defence of the pardoning of Mac Quirk, with remarks, p. 65.

Walpole Mr. his case supposed to be strictly in point to prove expulsion creates incapacity of being re-elected, v. i. p. 133 — the vote of expulsion as expressed in the votes, p. 143—remarks upon its meaning and extent, p. 145—the election was declared void, p. 147.

Weymouth lord, appointed one of the secretaries of state, v. i. p. 11—nominated to Ireland, p. 169.

Whittlebury-forest, the duke of Grafton hereditary ranger of, v. ii. p. 180—the right to the timber claimed by his grace, ib.

Wilkes Mr. his conduct often censured by Junius, v. i. p. 62—suffered to appear at large, and to canvas for the city and county, with an outlawry hanging over him, p. 68—his situation and private character gave the ministry advantages over him, p. 71—it is perhaps the greatest misfortune of his life that the duke of Grafton had so many compensations to make in the closet for his former friendship with him, p. 79—said more than moderate men would justify, p. 242—hardly serious at first, he became an enthusiast, p. 243 — commissions Mr. Thomas Walpole to solicit a pension for him, v. ii. p. 146—comes over from France to England, where he gets two hundred pounds from the duke of Portland and lord Rockingham, p. 147.

Woollaston Mr. expelled, re-elected, and admitted into the same parliament, v. i. p. 148—the public left to determine whether this be a plain matter of fact, p. 153.

Y.

Yates Mr. justice, quits the court of king's bench, v. ii. p. 47.

THE END.

www.ingramcontent.com/pod-product-compliance
Lightning Source LLC
Chambersburg PA
CBHW031856220426
43663CB00006B/645